ATTENTIVE
TO GOD

BEING AWARE OF GOD'S
PRESENCE IN DAILY LIFE

"*Through examples from the biblical narratives of Scripture, Tony has beautifully distilled for us how to practice listening to God in ordinary life.*"

Alfred Quah
Retreat and Spiritual Director of One Path (www.one-path.com)

"*For anyone who desires to go deeper with God and live closer to Him this book will be a great blessing. It is biblical, practical, and really helpful. It can be used individually or in a group and I warmly commend it.*"

Bishop Ken Clarke
Former Church of Ireland Bishop of Kilmore, Elphin and Ardagh

"*This is a warmly written, profoundly insightful and richly practical book. Tony's words have left me with a real hunger to be watchful for all the ways that God reaches out to me in my days; it's stirred up in me a greater longing to be responsive to God's touch so that I can know him more intimately, love him more deeply. I cannot recommend it highly enough.*"

Mags Duggan
Retreat Leader, Spiritual Director and
Author of *God among the Ruins* (BRF 2017)

"*Living in our urban city, we rush through our day without sensing God's ever-presence and call for us to be with Him. Attentive to God enables us to slow down and tune in to His presence, entering into a deep communion with God through all our senses.*"

Alvin Tan
Senior Pastor of Bartley Christian Church

"*An insightful book on being attentive to God by an inspiring man.*"

Alex Tang
Kairos Spiritual Formation (www.kairos2.com)

A Graceworks Publication by

TONY HORSFALL

ATTENTIVE
TO GOD

BEING AWARE OF GOD'S
PRESENCE IN DAILY LIFE

GRACEWORKS

Published by Graceworks Private Limited
22 Sin Ming Lane
#04-76 Midview City
Singapore 573969
Tel: 67523403
Email: enquiries@graceworks.com.sg
Website: www.graceworks.com.sg

ISBN: 978-981-11-5720-2

2 3 4 5 6 7 8 9 10 • 25 24 23 22 21 20 19

CONTENTS

Introduction   vii

Part 1 — Jacob, and the Problem of Inattentiveness (Genesis 28:10–22)

   1   Jacob's Story   1

   2   God's Presence — There is Nowhere He is Not   3

   3   Reasons for Inattentiveness   7

   4   The Grace of Divine Disclosure   11

   5   Living an Awakened Life   15

Spiritual Practice: Breathing Prayer   18

Part 2 — Moses, and the Importance of Turning Aside (Exodus 3:1–10)

   6   Moses' Story   23

   7   The Ordinary Made Special   26

   8   The Choice to Turn Aside   29

   9   Missing the Moment   32

  10   Encountering God   35

Spiritual Practice: The Prayer of Examen   38

Part 3 — Jeremiah, and the Gift of Seeing (Jeremiah 1:4–14)

  11   Jeremiah's Story   43

  12   The Word of the Lord Comes to Us   46

  13   Seeing Physically   50

14   Seeing Spiritually   54

15   Eyes to See?   59

Spiritual Practice: Awareness Walk   62

Part 4 — Samuel, and the Posture of Listening (1 Samuel 3:1–10)

16   Samuel's Story   67

17   Ears to Hear   70

18   The Posture of Listening   75

19   Incline Your Ear   80

20   Is That You God?   86

Spiritual Insight: Pierre de Caussade and the Sacrament of the Present Moment   90

Part 5 — Cleopas, and the Moment of Recognition (Luke 24:13–35)

21   Cleopas' Story   98

22   Poor Recognition   101

23   The Power of Friendship   105

24   The Opened Scriptures   109

25   The Breaking of Bread   115

Spiritual Insight: Brother Lawrence and Practising the Presence   122

Conclusion   125

Questions for Group Discussion   128

Notes   132

Bibliography   134

INTRODUCTION

One day at school I dreamed a dream. I dreamed I was a professional footballer, leading my team out for the Cup Final and scoring the winning goal. My mental reverie, however, came to an abrupt end when the teacher's voice broke into my consciousness, loud, insistent, and challenging.

"HORSFALL LAD, SIT UP STRAIGHT AND PAY ATTENTION!"

For a moment I was in shock, rendered speechless by this public humiliation. Somehow I managed to stammer a muted response of "Sorry sir", and with great effort began to re-focus my mind, trying to get to grips with the lesson.

Teachers of course know the importance of attentiveness in the learning process and are quick to remind their young charges of its necessity; pupils are generally much slower to grasp its significance, and often need reminding. Maybe it never happened to you quite like that but we all know how easy it is to lose concentration and let our attention wander. In the middle of talking to a friend, you suddenly realise you have not been listening at all and have lost the thread of the conversation because you were miles away. Or you are driving a familiar route but your mind is elsewhere so you miss your turn-off and are forced to make an unwelcomed detour simply because you were not concentrating on the road. It happens so easily, and far too frequently, this problem of inattentiveness.

It happens too in the spiritual life. God is speaking to us but we fail to recognise his voice. He has things to teach us, but our minds are elsewhere and we are not attuned to his whisper. He wants to lead us and guide us, but we miss his gentle promptings. He is present all around us, yet we don't notice his approach or register his nearness. We seem like Israel of old to be both blind and deaf to the overtures of God: "You have seen many things, but have paid no attention; your ears are open, but you hear nothing (Isaiah 42:20)."

Not only does our inattentiveness frustrate God, but it robs us of a greater depth in our relationship with him. We would enjoy a deeper intimacy with God if we were more attuned to him in our everyday lives. Moreover, we would have a clearer understanding of what he wanted us to do and be able to discern his will more easily. The purpose of this book is to help you become more consistently aware of God, to train your ear to hear his voice, and your eye to see what he is doing. Not that this is easy, or that I am myself an expert. I am a learner just as you are, and I have my own struggles with spiritual attentiveness, but I want to grow and improve so that I can serve God more effectively. I'm sure you do as well, which is why you are reading this book.

Although Jesus carefully chose his first disciples, the Twelve often proved to be slow learners and as slow to catch on as we are. On one occasion, shortly after the feeding of the 4,000, they were crossing the lake by boat when they realised they had forgotten to bring bread with them. They seemed unable to make the connection between the miracle they had just seen happen and the ability of Jesus to meet their needs. Jesus rebuked them with these words: "Do you have eyes but fail to see, and ears but fail to hear? And don't you remember (Mark 8:18)?" The significance of what had taken place had been lost on them because of their failure to see, to hear and to understand what was right there in front of them.

The disciples needed to wake up to the spiritual dimension all around them and to tune in to what God was doing in their midst. We contemporary disciples are no different. As Ben Campbell Johnson has said, "To be awake means to have our eyes opened so that we see, to have our ears opened so that we hear, to have our reason alert so that we understand. This is the biblical way of speaking about spiritual awareness."[1]

The shape of this book is built around five very familiar Bible stories in which we meet five individuals encountering God. Each story has something to teach us about moving from a lack of awareness of God to a place where we more readily recognise and respond to his presence. We will learn what it means to see with our eyes, to hear with our ears, and to have our minds opened to understand. Interspersed between the stories are some classical spiritual practices that can help us to develop and nurture our awareness, and some insights from church history that remind us that the desire to be more mindful of God is nothing new.

The chapters are deliberately short enough so that you can read them on a daily basis as part of your devotional practice over the course of a month. This steady reading over a period of time will produce better learning than dashing through the book as quickly as possible so you can add it to your "Books I have read this year" list. Read slowly, thoughtfully, and prayerfully. Above all, seek to put into practice what you are learning.

Additionally, there are questions for a small-group setting. These follow the five sections of the book and the idea is that you can share your journey of spiritual discovery with others if you wish. This of course is a great way to enhance your learning and deepen your experience. You will need to read the relevant chapters before your meeting and then be willing to share your findings with others. A group could meet weekly, fortnightly or even monthly.

So, now, with the help of the Holy Spirit and a prayer that God will make himself known to us more fully, we can begin our journey together into a greater awareness of God.

Reflection

As you begin working your way through this book why not pause for a moment and offer your own prayer to God. What do you want him to do for you as you read? If you have time, write out your prayer so you can turn to it again when you have finished reading, or even pray it at different moments as you read.

Part 1

Jacob, and the Problem of Inattentiveness

¹⁰ Jacob left Beersheba and set out for Harran. ¹¹ When he reached a certain place, he stopped for the night because the sun had set. Taking one of the stones there, he put it under his head and lay down to sleep. ¹² He had a dream in which he saw a stairway resting on the earth, with its top reaching to heaven, and the angels of God were ascending and descending on it. ¹³ There above it stood the LORD, and he said: "I am the LORD, the God of your father Abraham and the God of Isaac. I will give you and your descendants the land on which you are lying. ¹⁴ Your descendants will be like the dust of the earth, and you will spread out to the west and to the east, to the north and to the south. All peoples on earth will be blessed through you and your offspring. ¹⁵ I am with you and will watch over you wherever you go, and I will bring you back to this land. I will not leave you until I have done what I have promised you."

¹⁶ When Jacob awoke from his sleep, he thought, "Surely the LORD is in this place, and I was not aware of it." ¹⁷ He was afraid and said, "How awesome is this place! This is none other than the house of God; this is the gate of heaven."

¹⁸ Early the next morning Jacob took the stone he had placed under his head and set it up as a pillar and poured oil on top of it. ¹⁹ He called that place Bethel, though the city used to be called Luz.

²⁰ Then Jacob made a vow, saying, "If God will be with me and will watch over me on this journey I am taking and will give me food to eat and clothes to wear ²¹ so that I return safely to my father's household, then the LORD will be my God ²² and this stone that I have set up as a pillar will be God's house, and of all that you give me I will give you a tenth."

|1|

JACOB'S STORY

Jacob was part of what can only be described as a dysfunctional family, a family made dysfunctional by a passive, disinterested father (Isaac) and a mother (Rebekah) who favoured one son more than another.

Jacob had his own issues. He and his twin brother Esau were born in answer to prayer when it had appeared that Rebekah was barren (Genesis 25:21–26). Even in the womb there was a jostling for position between them, a rivalry that would intensify as they grew up. Jacob was born grasping his older brother's heel. His Hebrew name carries a reminder of this (Jacob means "he grasps the heel") and a suggestion that he was a grasper by nature, someone who would do whatever was necessary to get his own way and fulfil his ambitions. This is why Jacob is often described as a supplanter, a person who dispossesses another by dishonourable or treacherous means.

The two boys were as different as chalk and cheese. Esau, so called because of his red hair, loved the outdoors and became a skilled hunter, winning his father's admiration. Jacob was much quieter, a home bird who was closer to his mother and the apple of her eye. As the older son Esau had the greater birthright and stood in line to inherit their father's blessing, something Jacob coveted.

Jacob's calculating nature expressed itself early on when he tricked his brother into selling him his birthright. Esau had returned from the fields starving, and in a moment of madness swapped his birthright for a bowl of Jacob's stew. While the incident shows he did not value or appreciate his birthright (Hebrews 12:16–17), it also shows that Jacob was an opportunist ready to take whatever he wanted when the chance came.

Much later, when Isaac was an old man whose eyesight was failing, Jacob contrived with his mother to win his father's blessing. Urged on by Rebekah, he dressed as his brother in order to deceive Isaac who, having eaten and drunk, unwittingly prayed his prayer of blessing over the person he supposed was Esau. It was in fact Jacob, who had robbed his brother a second time. Esau was understandably furious, weeping for what he had lost, and swearing vengeance on his brother. Rebekah, realising the danger that Jacob was now in, urged her son to leave home and seek refuge with her brother Laban in Haran. So it was that the home-loving Jacob was forced into exile, fleeing for his life into the desert: "Jacob left Beersheba and set out for Haran (Genesis 28:10)."

This is the place where we meet Jacob in the story we are looking at, and he arrives there lonely, afraid and very unsure of his future. He has deceived his father, robbed his brother, and yet—scoundrel that he is—is still under the watchful eye of God, and destined to become an integral part of the divine purpose. Such is the grace of God. It is impossible to think of the story of Jacob without being reminded of the vastness of God's mercy or the depths of his love. We are reminded too that whatever our own family history, and whatever our past mistakes or wrong-doing, God waits to make himself known to us and to change and transform us even as he did the rascal Jacob. There is hope for us all.

Reflection

In what state do you find yourself as you begin reading?
Remember that the God of Jacob—the God of grace—welcomes you into his presence whatever your situation and need.

| 2 |

GOD'S PRESENCE — THERE IS NOWHERE HE IS NOT

In the mystery that is the providence of God, Jacob finds himself in the back of beyond, a place with no name and nothing to commend it, a desolate wilderness where there are no people, no buildings, and nothing is happening (v. 11). Yet this is the place to which God has brought him so that it may be a place of encounter and the beginning of personal transformation. To add to his sense of isolation and aloneness, the sun has set and darkness has descended. Enveloped in the gloom, Jacob stops to rest for the night, his surroundings representative of the bleakness within his inner landscape.

But where to lay his head? No shelter is available, so it will mean a night in the open, exposed to the elements and prey to wild animals. There is no comfort to be found either, and the only pillow available is a stone on which to lay his weary head. Ouch! Exhausted and drained he manages to fall asleep, and dreams a dream that will open up for him an understanding of the divine purpose for his life. He sees a stairway resting on the earth and reaching up to heaven where angels are ascending and descending. In the dream God speaks to him with promises about the future, for himself and all the descendants of Abraham. God has many ways by which he can reach us, and the subconscious is one of them. Dreams are often used by God to tell us what we fail to hear when we are awake. Stirred by what he has seen

Jacob wakes with the dream still vivid in his mind. "Surely the Lord is in this place," he says, "and I was not aware of it (v. 16)."

Wherever we find ourselves God is already there, for there is no place where he is not. The psalmist believed in the omnipresence of God, not as a philosophical idea or theological concept but as the reality behind his relationship with the divine: "Where can I go from your Spirit? Where can I flee from your presence? If I go up to heaven, you are there; if I make my bed in the depths, you are there. If I rise on the wings of the dawn, if I settle on the far side of the sea, even there your hand will guide me, your right hand will hold me fast (Psalm 139:7–10)." And perhaps most tellingly of all, given that we are thinking of Jacob's exile and his night spent in the desert, he continues: "If I say, 'Surely the darkness will hide me and the light become night around me,' even the darkness will not be dark to you; for the night will shine like the day, for darkness is as light to you (Psalm 139:11–12)." We can neither escape from God's presence nor inadvertently step out of it. Wherever we are, God is there and is waiting for us.

No matter where we find ourselves on planet earth we can say with certainty, "*Surely* the Lord is in *this* place." Like Jacob we may find ourselves in an unpromising geographical location that is without indication of God's presence or activity. It may appear to be a truly God-forsaken place, but it is not. We may, for example, be living in the midst of a culture that does not honour God, where demonic powers are strong and spiritual darkness rules, yet even there God is aware of us. To the church at Pergamum, a city drenched in paganism and idolatry, Jesus said, "I know where you live—where Satan has his throne (Revelation 2:13a)." God is mindful of us wherever we live: in a noisy, crowded high-rise apartment block; in a shanty town on the edge of a slum; in the high-pressured world of a metropolis. Wherever we are, God is there and we are never lost to his sight.

Like Jacob, we may find ourselves in an emotionally desolate place, cut off from friends and family, feeling unloved and abandoned, alone in the world. We may have suffered loss, felt the sting of bereavement, seen our dreams shattered and our hopes dashed, but even there God is present. Whatever our stage in life, whatever transition we may be going through, and whatever circumstances may befall us, we remain within the sphere of the divine nearness.

We may feel we are at a bad place spiritually, having failed yet again to live the life we are called to or to follow the spiritual practices that give us life. Our faith may be weak, our witness poor and our zeal flagging. We may have more doubts than certainties, more questions than answers. We may feel abandoned by God, and that we have lost the sense of his presence and favour, that our prayers are no longer heard. Yet however dark things seem, even there God is present. We are never cut adrift or left to our own devices.

The truth is, it is impossible to avoid the presence of God because there is no place where he is not. Where I am, God is already. Whether I realise it or not, I am always in his presence. The apostle Paul found wisdom in an ancient poet to underline his conviction that God is not far from any one of us: "For in him we live and move and have our being (Acts 17:27–28)." Our very existence takes place within the presence of God. Every breath that we breathe, every word that we speak, every movement we make, every word that we utter— everything happens within the parameters of God's presence. We are encircled by the divine, surrounded by the boundaries of grace.

C.S. Lewis wrote of this all-encompassing presence of God. He said, "We may ignore, but we can nowhere evade, the presence of God. The world is crowded with Him. He walks everywhere incognito. And the incognito is not always hard to penetrate. The real labour is to remember to attend. In fact, to come awake. Still more to remain awake."[2] Yes, there is sometimes a hiddenness about God. He does not always announce his presence with a fanfare of trumpets. He feels no need to broadcast his arrival or give notice of his coming. The Son of God himself entered our world incognito, as a babe born in the stable at Bethlehem—overlooked by most people despite ancient prophecies, angelic choirs and wondrous star. Only those with eyes to see and ears to hear, like the shepherds and the wise men, understood what was happening; the majority missed the moment of his appearance. And it is still the same today.

What we need then is, like Jacob, to awaken to God's presence, to develop a sensitivity to his nearness, and become more aware of his activity. The prophet Isaiah called to the people of his day: "Awake, awake, O Zion (Isaiah 52:1)" and the psalmist exhorted himself, "Awake my soul! Awake, harp and lyre! I will awaken the dawn (Psalm 57:8)." The church at Sardis is challenged with these stirring words: "Wake up! Strengthen what remains and is about to die (Revelation 3:2)." If we are to know God more deeply and be more effective in his service, we must stir our souls from slumber. We must come awake, and then stay awake.

The belief that God is all around us is foundational to our knowing him more fully. Wherever we find ourselves, we can say, "Surely the Lord is in *this* place", whether we are aware of him or not. With the conviction that the world is crowded with God firmly rooted in our hearts we can then begin to look for him in the ordinariness of our daily lives, knowing that he does not play hide and seek with us. As Lewis says, we can remember to attend, and awaken to his presence. God's promise remains true: if we seek for him with all our heart, then he will be found by us (Jeremiah 29:12–14).

Reflection

"There is no place where he is not." Ponder this truth and remind yourself that you can say with Jacob concerning the place you are in today, "Surely the Lord is in this place."

|3|

REASONS FOR INATTENTIVENESS

Jacob's admission was that he had been unaware of the presence of God. It is an admission that many of us in our overcrowded, distracted lives would have to make as well. What are the reasons behind our inattentiveness? And is our attention deficit something from which we can recover?

In his excellent book, *The Attentive Life*, Leighton Ford says that his own struggle with inattentiveness was a learned behaviour, a response he developed as he was growing up. Ford was adopted as a child, and his mother was a disciplinarian who often berated him at length. He admits that when he was young he simply switched off when she would scold him and developed a way of "tuning out" that affected him in other ways as well. Inattentiveness for him was a learned behaviour, a coping mechanism, and he is not alone in his tendency to tune out and not really listen.[3] However, if inattentiveness can be learned, so can attentiveness. To attend requires us to be able to focus our thinking and to choose not to be distracted. That takes some effort and a degree of practice before it becomes instinctive, but since it is a learned behaviour, it can be done.

As well as finding its origin in childhood experiences, inattentiveness is a by-product of living in a society where we suffer from information overload and where our senses are bombarded daily with an endless stream of visual and auditory messages. Our attention is continually being drawn away to other things. Mobile technology ensures that we are always in touch so there is no escape from the demands of email and messaging or the lure of internet surfing. The way we watch television encourages us to flick from channel to channel, dipping into several programmes simultaneously rather than becoming engrossed in one. The result of all this is that we are distracted and fragmented, pulled in many different directions at once, with little ability to focus on just one thing. Multi-tasking may be applauded, but it robs us of depth and concentration. To change this we will need to be more disciplined in our use of technology and train our minds to develop a single focus for our attention.

When we look at Jacob's inattentiveness, it was almost certainly to do with the fact that he was not expecting to encounter God. At that point in his life Jacob was not a spiritual person. His focus was on what we may call "carnal" matters, his thinking limited to earthly concerns and his personal ambitions (1 Corinthians 3:3). He wanted the status that the birthright would give him, and the blessing he sought was to do with material gain rather than spiritual growth. Despite being the grandson of Abraham, the great man of faith, he seems to have had little personal relationship with God, and was therefore not anticipating that God might speak to him. Indeed his shameful behaviour may have caused him to think that God would have no time for the scoundrel he knew himself to be.

God promises to reveal himself to us when we seek him with all our heart. If our lives are centred on material things, satisfying our physical desires and fulfilling personal ambitions, then the spiritual part of us will indeed be stifled. If we have no hunger for God, it is unlikely we will recognise his voice or be aware of his presence. To become more responsive to God we need to develop our spiritual dimension. As Paul puts it, "Those who live according to the sinful nature have their minds set on what that nature desires; but those who live in accordance with the Spirit have their minds set on what the Spirit desires (Romans 8:5)."

Another reason why Jacob was not responsive to God must have been the fact that he was preoccupied with his own concerns. His mind and his emotions were absorbed by the conflict with his brother, and the stress of being forced to leave home suddenly and against his will. No doubt he was all over the place emotionally and finding it hard to get his head together. The very word "pre-occupied" reminds us that where a space is occupied already, be it a house or a mind, there is little room for anyone or anything else. Jacob's mind was crowded and his heart congested; there was no space for God.

We have all experienced moments of self-absorption when it seems impossible to think about anything other than our particular concerns. Such self-absorption works against our spiritual progress and our knowing God more deeply. We may have to consciously adjust our thinking and bring our emotions under control so that we can pay attention to God and to other people, but this too is achievable. With a degree of self-discipline we can learn to focus on living in the present moment and taking notice of what is going on around us. And we can also learn to be more observant, to identify the signs of God's activity in our lives.

The good news is this: if Jacob could learn to become attentive to God, so can we. Yes, this requires discipline and application, and we will not be able to do it unaided, simply by willpower. We will need the help of God, but that help he is always willing to give. He is ready and waiting to heal our inattentiveness and bring wholeness to our fragmented souls if we would but ask him. Furthermore, he is also longing to reveal himself to us. It was in the grace of divine disclosure that Jacob discovered God's presence, and that is how we too will come to know his presence.

Reflection

What might be the reasons for your own inattentiveness?
Think carefully about what distracts you and consider how you might
overcome any propensity to lack focus.

The Grace of Divine Disclosure

No matter how attentive we are, or how disciplined we may be in seeking God, we are all dependent ultimately on the willingness of God to make himself known. It is a fact that God drew near to Jacob through his dream that opened the doorway for him into a deeper, more spiritual dimension to his life. God is always reaching out to us in love. The question is, "Are we reaching out to him in response?"

The Bible tells us that God is a God who speaks, who loves to communicate, and who has many channels of communication. The writer to the Hebrews reminds us, "In the past God spoke to our forefather through the prophets at many times and in various ways (Hebrews 1:1)." One common way was through a dream, and that was how God gained Jacob's attention. Jacob's dream was vivid and memorable, full of symbolism. What he saw was a ladder or staircase, connecting heaven with earth, and angels ascending and descending.

Some scholars suggest that what Jacob saw was a staircase with many steps, like the famous Ziggurat known to us from archaeology at Ur in the Chaldees. If this is so then the meaning of the dream is that there is a better and easier way to access God's presence than the upward climb or struggle associated with pagan worship.

Alternatively, Jacob may have seen an ordinary ladder and the point is that a connection was being made between heaven and earth; the gap was being bridged and relationship established. Either way, the dream suggests that it is God who is coming down to search for people rather than the other way around. The angels are busily moving up and down as they carry out the divine will on the earth, and the Lord is standing above the ladder as the One who is orchestrating everything and who is about to communicate. He seeks us out so that he may speak to us.

As we consider this matter of attentiveness to God it is important that we have clearly in our minds the fact that God wants to communicate with us, and that he takes the initiative to do so. He is no silent, remote, distant kind of a deity. He may not be a chatterbox (always talking), but he speaks often and clearly enough so that human beings may live in a relationship with him, and through prayer also enter into dialogue with him. This reality is something that the Old Testament prophets frequently emphasised to God's people. God, they said, is not like an idol who cannot hear or speak; he is neither deaf nor dumb. He is a living God, and he communicates to those who listen for his voice. It is vital that we believe this for ourselves. God speaks, and speaks to you, and you have the capacity to hear and recognise his voice.

So then, what is it that God says to Jacob? The message is absolutely one of grace, for it contains the promises of God for his chosen people that will now come to pass through Jacob. First of all, God introduces himself as the same God who had spoken to Jacob's relatives: he is the God of his grandfather Abraham and his father Isaac, and he will now be the God of Jacob too (v. 13). Then come the promises—of land (v. 13), many descendants (v. 14), blessing (v. 15), the divine presence (v. 15) and a future return to his homeland (v. 15). The emphasis throughout is on what God will do. This will come about in its entirety by divine action ("I will") and as a gift ("I will give you"). Jacob will be the recipient of blessings he has not earned or deserved. He will inherit the promises given to Abraham and Isaac. What is more, God himself will be the guarantee that everything will come to pass: "I will not leave you until I have done what I have promised you (v. 15)."

Jacob will now find himself carried along in the stream of God's purpose and God's guiding hand will be directing his steps until he returns once again to his homeland and the promises begin to be fulfilled. What strength that would have given him as he stepped into an unknown future! His destiny is now tied to the purpose of God, and in that he is secure. That God would so identify himself with a scoundrel like Jacob amazes us, but then we are all scoundrels in our own way. The only reason any of us receives anything from God is because he chooses to be gracious to us. He does so because it is his nature to be gracious, it is who he is, and his glory is seen not only in how he forgives our sins but also in how he takes us up into his plans and uses us to bring his purposes to pass.

One of the ways we can identify the voice of God is by the way he speaks—with love and grace. Yes, he may challenge and rebuke us when necessary, but the tone of his voice is never one that condemns us or leaves us without hope. This is how we can distinguish between the voice of God and the voice of the devil. Satan only ever speaks to bring us down, to make us feel miserable, to threaten and accuse us. His words are harsh and condemning, leaving us feeling thoroughly miserable, completely alone, and without hope. God on the other hand speaks to build us up, to encourage us, to motivate us to better things. His challenge comes with a promise, and his commands are for our good. After he has spoken, we feel strengthened, inspired and optimistic for the future. That was certainly the effect on Jacob.

What this means is that we should not be afraid of encountering God or hearing his voice. If we have the idea that God is out to get us, to find fault with us, or to lay heavy burdens on us we may well tune out and fail to pay attention. If, however, we know that when he speaks it will be for our good, we will welcome the possibility of encounter with anticipation and will actually seek God out, not hide away. We will long for the divine disclosure.

§

Reflection

Consider the fact that God in his love is always reaching out to you. What response do you wish to make to his overtures of grace?

| 5 |

LIVING AN AWAKENED LIFE

Jacob's encounter with God has an immediate and profound impact on him, which is not surprising. Any brush with the divine is going to leave its mark on us and has the potential to change us for ever. Jacob realises he has been on holy ground and exclaims, "How awesome is this place. This is none other than the house of God; this is the gate of heaven (v. 17)." Perhaps for the first time in his life he is awakened to the reality of God, and he responds accordingly.

Through the dream given to him by God, the dusty, dreary place where Jacob had laid down his head to sleep had been transformed for him into a sacred place, a place of interaction between earth and heaven. Without realising it, Jacob had camped himself where God was to be found and accidentally discovered a gateway to his presence. We are tempted to think that God's presence is locked into holy buildings, that he is to be found only in specially designated places, or confined to breath-taking locations; but Jacob's encounter reminds us that because there is no place where God is not present, even the most unlikely setting may turn out to be impregnated with the divine. It is simply a matter of awareness, of recognising what is already there, of waking up.

This realisation that the whole world is in fact the house of God, and that there are doorways into his presence all around us, gives us a new way of looking at our surroundings. We can expect to find God no matter where we are, and this expectation fires our faith that God is there right in the midst of our ordinary lives. He is there where we live, he is there where we work. He is there in our daily commute and as we do our weekly shopping; he is there when we change the baby, and when we do the washing-up. We live in a God-bathed world and, with a little practice and a measure of determination, we will find ourselves noticing his presence more and more, often where we least expect it.

If presence brings encounter, then encounter leads to worship. Jacob is unskilled in liturgical practice and the subtleties of worship services, but he responds instinctively with perhaps his first act of worship. It is simple, crude, but sincere. He takes the things that are there before him and uses them to express the sense of awe and wonder that has gripped his soul. Just as places can become sacred, so can objects. Jacob takes the stone pillar that had symbolised his separation, isolation and despair and makes an altar of it, standing it upright to represent what he now feels—recognition, acceptance, and possibility. Then he pours oil over it, perhaps symbolic of the grace that had flowed down upon him, perhaps representative of the Spirit and presence of God that had touched him. This is worship at its most pure—an uncluttered, instinctive response to the greatness of God. It is not sophistication that God looks for but sincerity; not complicated ritual but humble reality.

Next, Jacob names the place. In the Bible the naming of people and places, even of the animals, is significant for it is associated with the investing of character and potential. So Jacob names this out-of-the-way place Bethel, which means "house of God". The altar will stand as a memorial stone or marker, and will be the reminder to Jacob and others of what happened. He is looking to the future when according to God's promise he will return from exile and there will be the opportunity for Bethel to become a significant place in the worship of Israel (Genesis 31:13, 35:6–7, 14–15).

Finally, we see Jacob making a vow to God in response to the promises given to him. His words reveal that he is still a novice in spiritual terms and that he sees his relationship with God as something of a bargain to be negotiated. Transformation never happens overnight and most of us are in a state of flux spiritually—some aspects of our character are fully formed, others still need a lot of work. On the one hand we can see a confident expression of Jacob's faith, that God will provide for all his needs and bring him back safely to his own land. On the other hand we can see his tendency to look for the best deal possible. Will his commitment to God be determined by how well he feels God keeps his promises? And is his promise to give a tenth of all he receives from God the response of a generous heart, or a sort of investment that will bring further wealth? We cannot say for sure. All we do know is that Jacob has started a journey, not just a physical one that will bring him to his uncle Laban's house, but a spiritual one that will lead him to a deeper walk with God.

Being attentive to God is one of the foundation stones of the spiritual life. It is about awareness, recognition, watchfulness and noticing. Most of us are not naturally attentive. We are distracted and fragmented, and as such often fail to recognise God's presence in the midst of our daily lives. We can learn, though, how to be more attentive and we can develop a greater sensitivity to divine realities. Theologian Kevin Vanhoozer says that the Christian life is all about wakefulness: "If conversion is the moment of awakening to the reality of God, discipleship is the effort we make to stay awake."[4] That may give a new slant to our discipleship and it is the theme that we shall now continue to explore.

Reflection

"The whole world is in fact the house of God." This was Jacob's discovery, and it can be yours as well. Ask God to show you the gateways into his presence that can be found right where you are, in the ordinariness of your daily life. You too can live an awakened life.

Spiritual Practice

Breathing Prayer

One of the ways by which we can become more attentive and less distracted is to learn how to pray to the rhythm of our breathing. This simple practice helps us to become more centred within ourselves, and therefore better able to focus on God. It is an essential part of slowing down and becoming more attuned to the spiritual dimension of life.

The Bible gives a special significance to breathing, since it is associated with life itself. See Genesis 2:7, Acts 17:25, John 20:22. God has given us the breath of life, and to become prayerfully conscious of one's breathing, is in fact to become conscious of the God who created us and is breathing his life into us. The Hebrew word for Spirit is *ruach*, which also means breath.

A good way of praying is simply to make yourself feel conscious of your breathing and to feel God's Spirit being infused into you, natural and supernatural life being inflated into one simultaneously.

Slow down your breathing. Breathe slowly and deliberately.

As you breathe in, the Spirit of God is being imparted to you. Receive the Spirit.

As you breathe out, you are expressing your partnership with the Spirit and allowing him to work through you. Let go of all struggle and striving and yield yourself to God.

As we breathe in we receive.

As we breathe out we let go.

By breathing prayerfully, without words, we are reminding ourselves of the miracle of our creation (and the gift of life), as well as the indwelling of the Holy Spirit (and the gift of new life).

This form of prayer can be combined with words such as **the Jesus Prayer**, an ancient way of concentrating on God, in order to become more aware of spiritual realities.

Lord Jesus Christ	*Breathe in*
Son of God	*Breathe out*
Have mercy on me	*Breathe in*
A sinner	*Breathe out*

You can also pray this prayer as you walk, slowly and thoughtfully, at any time during the day. It will slow you down and calm your spirit, making you more receptive to God. Pray for 5–10 minutes in this way on a regular basis to gain most benefit.

It is an excellent way of relaxing yourself as well. I often find myself using it in the middle of the night when I wake with anxious thoughts. It helps me to recalibrate my mind from fear to trust, and to focus on God not myself. At first it may be a struggle to concentrate, but when we persevere we usually find a sense of peace and can sleep again.

If you wish, you can use your own simple form of words such as *Abba, Father,* or *Jesus, Lord.* Any simple expression of love and devotion that fits the rhythm of your breathing can be used. Be creative and don't be afraid to experiment. Remember, the goal is to become more attentive, more aware. ✣

Part 2

Moses, and the Importance of Turning Aside

¹ Now Moses was tending the flock of Jethro his father-in-law, the priest of Midian, and he led the flock to the far side of the wilderness and came to Horeb, the mountain of God. ² There the angel of the Lord appeared to him in flames of fire from within a bush. Moses saw that though the bush was on fire it did not burn up. ³ So Moses thought, "I will go over and see this strange sight—why the bush does not burn up."

⁴ When the Lord saw that he had gone over to look, God called to him from within the bush, "Moses! Moses!"

And Moses said, "Here I am."

⁵ "Do not come any closer," God said. "Take off your sandals, for the place where you are standing is holy ground." ⁶ Then he said, "I am the God of your father, the God of Abraham, the God of Isaac and the God of Jacob." At this, Moses hid his face, because he was afraid to look at God.

⁷ The Lord said, "I have indeed seen the misery of my people in Egypt. I have heard them crying out because of their slave drivers, and I am concerned about their suffering. ⁸ So I have come down to rescue them from the hand of the Egyptians and to bring them up out of that land into a good and spacious land, a land flowing with milk and honey—the home of the Canaanites, Hittites, Amorites, Perizzites, Hivites and Jebusites. ⁹ And now the cry of the Israelites has reached me, and I have seen the way the Egyptians are oppressing them. ¹⁰ So now, go. I am sending you to Pharaoh to bring my people the Israelites out of Egypt."

|6|

MOSES' STORY

Moses is one of the great figures of the Old Testament, the man responsible for leading the people of Israel out of their slavery in Egypt and for giving them the Law. He lived to be 120 years old and it is noted that even in his later years his eyesight was still good and he walked with a spring in his step (Deuteronomy 34:7). His life has often been summed up in this way: the first 40 years he spent thinking he was a somebody; the second 40 years realising he was a nobody; and the final 40 years seeing what God could do with that nobody.

The providence of God can be seen clearly in his early years. Moses was born at a time when the people of Israel were enslaved in Egypt and Pharaoh feared that their growing numbers were becoming a threat to his country. He gave an order that any Israelite baby boy was to be thrown into the Nile. With great courage his mother kept him hidden for three months, but when they could conceal his presence no longer, she placed him in a papyrus basket and hid him among the reeds by the banks of the Nile. His sister Miriam was watching from a safe distance.

It happened that Pharaoh's daughter came down to bathe at that time, and discovered the child. Recognising it to be a Hebrew baby, she had compassion on the child and sent for one of the Hebrew women to nurse him. The woman chosen was his real mother, and she found herself being paid to care for her own baby! When the child had grown, he was taken into Pharaoh's court and raised by his daughter. She gave him the name Moses, which sounds in Hebrew like "drawn out", a reminder of how he had been drawn out of the water. Thus Moses, a Hebrew born into slavery, was given a privileged upbringing and a fine education. Surrounded by such wealth and status, it is not surprising he began to think of himself as a "somebody".

Moses, however, in addition to his pride, had something of an identity crisis as he came into manhood. Although raised as an Egyptian, he was a Hebrew at heart, and could not bear to see how his own people were being treated. One day he saw an Egyptian beating a Hebrew slave and he intervened, killing the Egyptian in his rage and then hiding his body. It was an act of presumption born out of arrogance. His crime had been seen, though, and when Pharaoh heard of it he tried to kill Moses, which meant Moses had to flee for his life. Like Jacob, he found himself in exile, and there in the desert of Midian, stripped of his position and privilege and reduced to tending sheep in the desert, he began to realise he was in fact a "nobody".

The middle period of his life spent in Midian was a wilderness time for Moses with long years spent in obscurity and seemingly very little of significance happening. I wonder how often Moses felt he was wasting his life, and how often he asked himself, "What am I doing here?" Moses was being humbled and prepared for things yet to happen, although he had no idea of what God had planned for him. He met and married Zipporah, the daughter of Reuel (better known as Jethro), and they had a son whom they named Gershom. The name summed up his feelings. It means "I have become an alien in a foreign land". Moses spent his days caring for his father-in-law's sheep, a lonely and boring job for one so well-schooled.

Meanwhile in Egypt, the people of Israel were suffering even more under the oppression of the Egyptians, and their cries for help were heard by God. The time had come for divine intervention so that the covenant promises given to Abraham, Isaac and Jacob, could come to pass. God was about to act to rescue his people and Moses was the man he had prepared to lead his people out of their bondage. He was about to learn what God can do with a "nobody", and in the timetable of God to experience something that will change the whole direction of his life.

There is encouragement here for us all. The providence of God is at work in the life of every believer, and God is preparing us today for what he wants us to do tomorrow. Nothing is wasted in God's economy. Whatever our upbringing, be it good or bad, God uses it to form and shape us for future service. Even our times of apparent failure, barrenness or isolation are powerful forces in the way God prepares us so that we can be used by him. We too may have to be humbled like Moses in order to discover what God can do with a "nobody". It may feel like nothing much is happening, but we can be sure that in God's time his purpose for us will come to pass and he will make himself known to us.

※

Reflection

How have you seen the providence of God at work in your own life?
How has God been at work to shape you and to smoothen your
rough edges?

| 7 |

THE ORDINARY MADE SPECIAL

We last saw Moses doing what he has done for the last several years, tending his father's sheep in a remote part of the desert (v. 3). His exciting life in the courts of Pharaoh now seems a million miles away and he has resigned himself to the mundane life of a shepherd. Every day is the same. He leads the flock out in the morning to find whatever water or pasture there is, watches over them to protect them from wild animals, then settles them down for the night. It is a humdrum, mediocre existence, going nowhere, amounting to very little. This was not what he had dreamed of as a boy, but it had become the reality of his existence, and this day was like any other day—ordinary.

We do not like the ordinary. The ordinary seems boring, of little value, something to be despised. We look for the exciting, the stimulating, that which is novel or new. We crave that which is exhilarating, original, and trendy. We disregard that which is common-place, familiar, unremarkable. The world in which we live is continually telling us to look for the extraordinary and to be dissatisfied with that which is simply routine. We must move from one amazing event to another, and our lives must suggest that every day is remarkable. Take a glance at social media: special is what matters, run-of-the mill doesn't count.

Not surprisingly, this trend carries over into our approach to the Christian life and what we expect from church. We tend to think that God is to be found most easily in the spectacular. So we look for the miraculous, the supernatural, the dramatic, and if these are absent we feel let down. If our church gatherings are not awesome, brilliant or mega exciting we assume we are failing in some way and that God is not with us. Nothing could be further from the truth. Yes, we do see heaven breaking through occasionally, and it is right to long for more, but we must remember that when God came to earth it was as a baby hidden in a cattle shed. Most of those in Bethlehem that night missed what was happening simply because one of the most miraculous events that ever took place was actually quite unspectacular to human eyes. God is not always in the extraordinary. Often he is in the common-place.

In the calendar of the Christian year which is followed by many major denominations, there is a huge period of time designated as "Ordinary Time". It occurs in two sections, one between Epiphany and Lent, and the other much longer section between Pentecost and Advent. The calendar rightly encourages us to celebrate the major Christian festivals as special occasions worthy of note; but it also recognises there are long periods of time when apparently not much is happening. This reminds us that discipleship is as much about steady faithfulness in the daily routines of life as it is about special events and happenings. When the psalmist tells us to "number our days (Psalm 90:12)" he surely means that we are to value each and every day, not just red-letter days when something special happens.

The reality is that much of life is ordinary, and we all have long periods when nothing much seems to be happening and we find ourselves engaged with the mundane tasks of everyday living. What is more, most of us are ordinary people. We are not outstandingly gifted, unusually attractive, or especially noteworthy. We don't make the headlines or have a high profile. Nothing about us is out of the ordinary and we walk down the street unnoticed. If we fail to appreciate or fail to be content with ordinariness we will feel disappointed and cheated. Yet here is the paradox. God can be found in the ordinary, and the ordinary can be made special. God appeared to Moses as he was going about his daily business. He came to him in the most unlikely of places, and when he was least expecting it, and that is where he is likely to come to us also.

It was the same when Jesus called his first disciples, ordinary fisherman from a Galilean backwater. He found Simon and Andrew about to cast their net into the lake, doing what they did every day, following the routine of a lifetime. Nearby he saw James and John, mending their nets (what a chore!) and getting ready to fish. Ordinary people doing ordinary things on an ordinary day. Yet to all four he called out "Come and follow me," which they did, leaving their family and work behind to join his mentoring programme (Mark 1:16–20). Life would never be the same again for any of them.

This means we need to develop what theologian Dr Paula Gooder calls a "spirituality of ordinariness". So often we miss glimpses of God's glory, not because they are not there but because we fail to notice them. She says that "we need to learn to be self-confidently 'ordinary' people who can celebrate God in the ordinary things of life, who can look for and encounter God in the everyday, who expect God to meet us while we wash up, get on the train or talk to friends. We need to be alert to the possibility that this event or that encounter might just provide us with a glimpse of glory."[5]

Don't be fooled by the ordinariness of your life, and don't think that God is not there because nothing spectacular seems to be happening. Keep watching for evidence of his presence and if you are patient in due time you will be rewarded.

Reflection

Are you tempted to despise the ordinary? If so, ask God to help you see the evidence of his presence in the humdrum of your daily life.

| 8 |

THE CHOICE TO TURN ASIDE

Into the ordinariness of his life as a shepherd in the desert of Midian God now reveals himself to Moses. He is tending the sheep as usual, perhaps lost in his own thoughts, maybe calculating the route he needs to take with his flock, when suddenly his attention is caught by an unusual sight—a bush is on fire, and yet it is not burnt up.

I like to think of God as the great Attention Grabber. He loves to break into our self-contained little worlds and remind us that he is there, awakening us to his nearness and prodding us into the consciousness of his reality. He does this in a number of ways, often taking us by surprise and catching our attention with something unusual, that we didn't expect, like this burning bush. We can't fail to notice such happenings and we are challenged to make sense of what we experienced. Often these events occur as something unusual, perhaps a surprising coincidence or an incredibly timely meeting, and often with a touch of humour too. They make their mark on us and bring us to life, like a splash of cold water on the face. We can't avoid noticing them, and like a tap on the shoulder we instinctively turn round.

In his book *The Reflective Life*, writer Ken Gire encourages us to become more aware of such happenings. "The reflective life," he says, "is a life that is attentive, receptive, and responsive to what God is doing in us and around us."[6] He encourages us to develop three habits of heart that will help us to unpack what God may be saying to us as he grabs our attention:

1. Read the moment—that is, recognise that this is indeed not just a coincidence or an interesting event, but something through which God is calling to us.

2. Reflect on the moment—take time to consider how and why God is addressing us, and find the meaning in what has taken place.

3. Respond to the moment—if this is God, then we must respond to his invitation in a way that is appropriate, perhaps with obedience, faith or love.

If we review our lives all of us will be able to remember such moments of connection with God. Once we begin to register that this is indeed how God works we will become more adept at recognising them for ourselves. All it requires is the discipline to notice and the faith to respond.

What struck Moses was not that the bush was on fire, but that it was not consumed (v. 2). The spontaneous combustion of scrub in the desert is a common occurrence, and therefore not so unusual, but as any scientist knows, where there is combustion something is being consumed. So a bush on fire is normally quickly reduced to ashes. This bush, in contradiction to that, continued to burn without being destroyed. His curiosity aroused, Moses makes a choice to go over and take a closer look: "I will go over and see this strange sight—why the bush does not burn up (v. 3)." He was intrigued, and recognised the moment as special.

Rather than getting on with his journey Moses chooses to turn aside. The Hebrew word translated here as "go over" carries the idea of stepping off a pre-determined path. Moses had his plans for the day, and an idea of what he wanted to accomplish, but he was willing to put his own schedule to one side in order to learn more. Our inflexibility often robs us of these holy moments, for we can be prisoners to our own objectives. Moses, however, displays a holy curiosity to know more and an openness to that which had grabbed his attention. He is willing to waste some time in order to explore what is going on.

This willingness to be diverted by the divine is itself a quality to be nurtured in our life with God. As Ruth Hayley Barton says, "The practice of 'turning aside to look' is a spiritual discipline that by its very nature sets us up for encounter with God . . . If spiritual leadership is anything, it is the capacity to see the burning bush in the middle of our own life and having enough sense to turn aside, take off our shoes and pay attention."[7] Yet it is always a choice, and choice suggests that there are other alternatives. There is so much to be done. We have our schedules to keep, our agendas to follow. Do we have the time to stop and register a God moment? Can we afford such a luxury in our overcrowded lives?

How we answer will largely determine how deeply we are able to grow in God and how well we get to understand his ways.

※

Reflection

Where have the God moments been in your life during the past week?
Did you step aside, like Moses, to engage with God or merely pass by?
What do you learn from this?

| 9 |

MISSING THE MOMENT

Moses must have felt the pressure to continue on his journey and to keep to his schedule, but in that moment of decision he chose to turn aside and to explore further the mystery of the burning bush. It may have seemed like an inconsequential thing to do, but it would have far-reaching implications for his life. God was waiting to speak to him, seeking his attention: "When the Lord saw that he had gone over to look, God called to him from within the bush, 'Moses! Moses!' (v. 4)." The moment of encounter would become the moment of his calling.

The compassionate God of Israel has heard the cries of his people. He is aware of their suffering at the hands of their Egyptian overlords, and he is about to act to rescue them. He is going to act on their behalf to release them from slavery and bring them into the land he had promised to give their forefathers. It is a significant moment in the history of God's people, and Moses is to be at the heart of what God will do. He will be the one to lead them out of Egypt. His whole life has been a preparation for this moment, and he could so easily have missed it had he not chosen to turn aside.

We remember the story that Jesus told of the Good Samaritan. The priest and the Levite both missed the opportunity to help a man in need. They were so busy doing their religious duties that they failed to recognise the one thing God wanted them to do—to stop and help the man who had been attacked. It was a passing Samaritan who chose to stop and be inconvenienced by offering help and support to the victim of robbery. He alone recognised the moment and responded with mercy. The others failed to see, their eyes blinded by their own agendas. Ironic, isn't it, that our very focus on service of God can sometimes cause us to miss a God-given opportunity?

There is no doubt that busyness must be one of the main reasons why we often miss the moment of God's approach. We have many things to do, all of them worthwhile, and all of them important. We have no time to stop, we have no time to spare. Our schedules are crowded, our diaries full, and we like it that way. It makes us feel important, wanted, valued, as if we must be achieving something. It also means that we cannot stop when we need to, that sometimes we don't notice what God is doing even when it is right before our eyes. That is the price many of us pay for being overcommitted.

The 'hurry sickness' that plagues our lives also robs us of our attentiveness. We live at such a pace that we no longer see our surroundings. Everything passes by in a blur. We are hurrying, scurrying our way through life with no way to slow down, let alone to attend to anything outside our self-established parameters. This blinkered living may help us to achieve our own goals, but may inadvertently cause us to miss those that matter to God.

If God is often to be found in the ordinary, in the hidden, in the lowly, then we will need to slow down. Only then will we truly experience the sacred moments in our everyday lives, and be able to engage with those people through whom God will make himself known to us. American writer Barbara Brown Taylor says, "The practice of paying attention really does take time. . . . Reverence requires a certain pace. It requires a willingness to take detours, even side trips, which are not part of the original plan."[8] Here is a choice we all have to make, between continuing to live life at full throttle and deciding to live at a steadier, more sustainable pace that allows us to become more reflective. That is a choice you and I must make for ourselves. No-one else can do that for us. We must be careful not to miss the moment of God's nearness.

❧

Reflection

How would you describe the pace of your life? Are you constantly living at full throttle and in danger of missing the activity of God? Have you enough capacity to be able to slow down and be more reflective?

|10|

Encountering God

Moses has been called to turn aside so that God may have his full attention. The burning bush is there simply to catch his eye and arouse his curiosity. The Lord will now speak to him from within the bush for this desert shrub is in fact aflame with the fiery presence of God.

Moses is called by name, and called twice, as are so many of the servants of God in the Bible. It is always encouraging when someone knows our name, especially when that someone is important to us. The truth that God knows us by name—that is with intimate, personal knowledge—is most amazing. It means he is aware of us, takes thought for us and wants to address us. Moses responds in the way that so many others have done when confronted with the presence of God. Three simple words are sufficient to communicate his heart response: "Here I am" (v. 4). They are words that speak of availability, surrender and co-operation. They sum up the reaction God is looking for from each of us.

As welcome as Moses is in the divine presence there is a sense of propriety that must be kept. This is after all the Lord God Almighty, the trice holy God, and it is better that Moses does not overstep the mark. Rather he is told, "Take off your sandals, for the place where you are standing is holy ground (v. 5)." This piece of desert scrubland, this scrap of sandy wilderness where sheep have grazed and left their mark, has been transformed into holy ground. The common has indeed been made holy by the presence of God, and Moses is called to respond appropriately.

Without doubt, his shoes would have been dirty, contaminated by sheep dung and whatever else had attached itself to him as he wandered the desert. The removal of his shoes represents a separation from sin and the defilement of living in the world, the sin that so easily entangles us (Hebrews 12:1). In many cultures it is customary to take off one's shoes before entering a house so as not to bring the dirt from outside into the sanctuary of the home. Likewise, whenever we draw near to God it is appropriate to cleanse our hearts as we enter his holy presence (Hebrews 10:22).

The reason we wear shoes of course is to protect our feet. Taking off one's shoes therefore implies a degree of vulnerability. Whenever we come before God there is the prospect not only of experiencing pleasure, but also pain. Transformation does not happen without our being open to the touch of God and confronted with our need to change. Being barefoot also implies a certain humility as well for it brings us into direct contact with the soil. Humus is the name given to the organic component of soil that is formed by the decomposition of leaves and other plant material, and it is from this word that humility and humanity are derived. In any true encounter with God we will be made to feel again our humanness, and we may well be brought low and know what it is to be humbled.

When God speaks he first introduces himself and then shares his purpose. Who is the One who speaks from within the bush? It is the God of the covenant, the God of his ancestors—the God who befriended Abraham, Isaac and Jacob and made known his purposes to them. During the time of Israel's slavery, the promises have not been forgotten. Now he is about to act in sovereign power. Notice the string of statements about God that link Moses inextricably with the purpose of God: I have seen—I have heard—I am concerned—I have come down—I am sending you. Far from having been discarded by God, Moses has been prepared for this moment. He has not been cast aside or forgotten during his exile in Midian. He has been made ready for the most important part of his life, when he will see what God can do with a "nobody".

Almost always, God chooses to accomplish his ends through human means. He could of course do things without us, and he might choose to use angels, but more often than not God's purposes are brought to pass through people who are available for God to use. "So now go," says the Lord, "I am sending you to Pharaoh to bring my people the Israelites out of Egypt (v. 10)." Moses will become integral to what God is going to do for his people and this has come about because he was willing to turn aside and in so doing encounter God.

We must never underestimate the significance of God's interventions in our own lives. When the great Attention Grabber gives us a prod, even when we least expect it or it seems a little inconvenient, we must be ready to respond with alacrity, and like Moses offer ourselves to God with the simple words, "Here I am." Our willingness to turn aside in such key moments will make all the difference in the satisfying of our desire to know God more deeply and in the fulfilment of our longing to be used by him.

※

Reflection

How has God been seeking to grab your attention recently?
What do you think he may be saying to you?

SPIRITUAL PRACTICE

The Prayer of Examen

A great way to pray and become more attentive is to look for God's presence in your daily life. More than 400 years ago Saint Ignatius encouraged what has been called prayer-filled mindfulness by teaching his followers the Prayer of Examen. It is a way of reflecting on what is happening in our lives, a way of stepping aside like Moses, in order to give full attention to what God is doing. Essentially, we are asking "Where was God in my day?" It is best done at the close of the day, and it can be adapted in ways that best suit your needs—it is not a rigid formula, but a spiritual habit that can be cultivated to aid our attentiveness.

Think back over the last 24 hours, or if you prefer, the last 2–3 days. Replay the events in your mind, like a video recording. Try to do this in chronological order. You may need to go over this several times, and to make simple notes of all that took place.

The question: Where can you discern the activity of God in your life during this period?

> Were there moments when you were led by God?
> When you heard the prompting of his Spirit?
> When you were conscious of God's presence, or moved to worship?
> Can you see evidence of God's provision? Of his protection? Of his goodness?
>
> *Give thanks for his working in you.*

Can you identify occasions when God was working through you?

When you produced the fruit of the Spirit? Love, joy, peace, patience....

When you did something that was an expression of your faith? An act of kindness....

When you were able to share your faith with another person?

When you were moved to pray?

When you felt the pull of temptation, but by God's grace resisted?

Give thanks for his working in you.

Are you aware of moments when you may have made mistakes, or sinned?

Is there anything that you regret?

Did you miss opportunities to live out your faith?

Were there times when you became anxious, worried or afraid?

What difficulties did you encounter? What problems emerged?

Where was God calling you to trust him?

Give thanks for his working in you, for his forgiveness, and nearness in times of trouble.

Is there anything that you would like to do tomorrow (or in the near future) as a result of this review of your life? Bring it before God, asking him for the grace to turn desire into action.

Clearly that kind of review needs a good amount of time, so it will not be easy to practice that on a daily basis. A much shorter format is at the end of the day to simply ask yourself the question "For what am I grateful today?" and then allow the Holy Spirit to remind you of all that has happened and the things for which you can then give thanks to God. This is a great way to finish off your day and to be reminded of God's presence in your life. Again, you can be creative in the way you practice this form of prayer and adapt it to your own needs. 🌿

Part 3

JEREMIAH, AND THE GIFT OF SEEING

⁴ The word of the Lord came to me, saying,

⁵ "Before I formed you in the womb I knew you,
  before you were born I set you apart;
  I appointed you as a prophet to the nations."

⁶ "Alas, Sovereign Lord," I said, "I do not know how to speak; I am too young."

⁷ But the Lord said to me, "Do not say, 'I am too young.' You must go to everyone I send you to and say whatever I command you. ⁸ Do not be afraid of them, for I am with you and will rescue you," declares the Lord.

⁹ Then the Lord reached out his hand and touched my mouth and said to me, "I have put my words in your mouth. ¹⁰ See, today I appoint you over nations and kingdoms to uproot and tear down, to destroy and overthrow, to build and to plant."

¹¹ The word of the Lord came to me: "What do you see, Jeremiah?"

"I see the branch of an almond tree," I replied.

¹² The Lord said to me, "You have seen correctly, for I am watching to see that my word is fulfilled."

¹³ The word of the Lord came to me again: "What do you see?"

"I see a pot that is boiling," I answered. "It is tilting toward us from the north."

¹⁴ The Lord said to me, "From the north disaster will be poured out on all who live in the land."

11

JEREMIAH'S STORY

Jeremiah grew up in a priestly family, and as a young man was called by God to be a prophet. His ministry covered a period of 40 years (626–586 BC) during some of the darkest days of Israel's history, from the time of King Josiah to the time of the Babylonian exile. He has been called the prophet of Judah's midnight hour because he ministered in such troubled times, and the weeping prophet because he found it so emotionally painful to deliver the message of judgement he had been given.

A prophet is someone skilled in hearing the word of God and then sharing what has been received with others. Four times in this passage we are told that the word of the Lord came to Jeremiah (vv. 2, 4, 11, 13). God is a God who speaks, and his word finds us wherever we may be. It comes to us and addresses us as if by name and Jeremiah found there was no hiding place from the voice of God. Prophets are also those who are able to perceive spiritual truth, they are able to see what others fail to recognise, which is why they were also known in Old Testament days as "seers". Jeremiah often received God's word through what he saw, both physically and spiritually, and here we are told how Jeremiah learned to develop this ability.

God's commission to Jeremiah begins with the encouragement that he has been prepared beforehand for the task of being a prophet to the nations. This preparation went back in time to before he had even been conceived, and continued as he was formed by God in his mother's womb. He had been set apart by God from birth, and was now being appointed to a specific calling, to speak on behalf of God to the nations (vv. 4–5). God knew Jeremiah intimately and gave him a work to do for which he was uniquely created, even though it was to be a hard and difficult calling.

By personality Jeremiah appears to have been a sensitive soul, but this very sensitivity enabled him to feel the message he had to deliver. His love for God and his love for God's people created deep emotional turmoil within him that reflected the heart of God. A message as strong on judgement as the one he was to deliver in Jerusalem could only be spoken through a broken heart. As one writer says, "He did not merely speak *for* God; he felt *with* Him; and he did not merely speak to the people; he felt *with* them"[9] (his italics).

Like many of us, Jeremiah felt inadequate for the task ahead of him, in particular because he was so young and unskilled at speaking. Youthfulness is no barrier to God however, and his excuse is rejected (vv. 6–7). Two reassurances are given to the teenage prophet-in-the-making. Firstly, God will be with him so there is no need to fear (v. 8). Secondly, he will be given the words to say (v. 9). His appointment is validated by God and that will give him sufficient authority no matter where he is sent (v. 10).

As we grow in our attentiveness to God we will learn how to recognise and hear the voice of God and how to develop the spiritual gift of seeing. Jeremiah is asked twice by God, "What do you see? (vv. 11, 13)." We will discover that God speaks to us through what we see, whether literally though our natural eyes, or figuratively through the eyes of our hearts. This means that we need to walk through the world with our eyes wide open, noticing what is around us and becoming more aware of the impressions God is giving us in our spirits. This will become one of the main ways by which we receive the word of God for ourselves and to share with others.

Reflection

How would you describe your personality?
How does it impact the way you relate to God?

| 12 |

THE WORD OF THE LORD COMES TO US

We have already mentioned that the expression "the word of the Lord came to me" occurs four times in the account of Jeremiah's call to the prophetic ministry. It is a significant expression because it opens for us the possibility that God will speak to us as well. It is clear from this saying that God is a God who speaks to his people. He does not sit aloof in heaven, silent and withdrawn. He is neither stand-offish nor remote but engages with his people and communicates with them when the time is right. This is surely encouragement for all of us who long for a deeper relationship with the living God.

The fact that God speaks is one of the great revelations of the Old Testament and a truth that distinguished the God of Israel from the deities worshipped by other peoples. The prophets were especially scathing in their denunciations of the idols venerated in surrounding nations. Such man-made objects were made of wood that rotted, had to be carried around because they could not walk, and nailed down to stop them from toppling over. They were worthless and useless. Jeremiah himself made the point: "Like a scarecrow in a melon patch, their idols cannot speak; they must be carried because they cannot walk (Jeremiah 10:5)." By contrast Israel's God was alive and active, powerful and involved: "But the Lord is the true God; he is the living God, the eternal King (Jeremiah 10:10)." Created objects can never compare with the Creator!

This understanding of a God who speaks is crucial to our belief that we can grow in spiritual awareness. We do not have a silent God who is detached from the world. For a long time my own concept of God was that he was distant and uncommunicative. I didn't expect him to speak to me, except perhaps when I died, and then hopefully he might say "Well done, good and faithful servant", but I wasn't too sure about even that. Only later as my idea of God was healed and my mind renewed did I begin to conceive of a Father God who loves to encourage his children and speak of his love for them. Jeremiah had no such blockage. He knew that God could speak to him.

Notice that the word of the Lord came to Jeremiah. The movement was from heaven to earth, from God to his people. This reminds us that the initiative is with God. He chooses to speak and sends forth his word to accomplish his purpose, and it is an act of grace. We do not make it happen. That word seeks us and finds us, and all we can do is to welcome it and receive it so that it can do its work in our lives. Isaiah describes this process in some detail: "As the rain and snow come down from heaven, and do not return to it without watering the earth and making it bud and flourish, so that it yields seed for the sower and bread for the eater, so is my word that goes out from my mouth: It will not return to me empty, but will accomplish what I desire and achieve the purpose for which I sent it (Isaiah 55:10–11)."

From these verses we can draw several conclusions. Firstly, the word of God comes to us as and when God chooses to send it. Just as we cannot control the weather, neither can we control when or how God will speak. All we know is that he will, in his own good time. Secondly, when the word comes it is life-giving and nourishing to the soul, just as rain and snow water the earth and cause growth to happen in the natural world. The word from God is always productive. Thirdly, the word of God is given for a reason and for a purpose, and is effective in achieving God's aim. It comes to us with power and brings its own authentication.

Of course, we have a part to play in this process. We must welcome and receive the word and our hearts must be like well-prepared, fertile ground (Matthew 13:23). We are to respond to it with faith (believing what we hear) and with obedience (doing what he tells us to do), then it will be productive in our lives too (Hebrews 4:2, James 1:22). This is how we grow in grace and are transformed.

As we consider the call of Jeremiah, we can identify several key principles to guide us as we go forward:

1. God is a God who speaks today. He is alive and active in the world he has made and wants to communicate with people.

2. God speaks to us personally, and to ordinary people like us, in the midst of our ordinary lives. Jeremiah was a country boy, and still quite young, yet the word of the Lord found him there in quiet Anathoth and addressed him by name. We are not to think that we are unnoticed by God or of no importance to him. He will speak to us where we are and we will be able to hear his voice.

3. God speaks in order to strengthen and encourage us for the work he has for us to do. He has a purpose for every life but does not leave us to struggle alone. When we need help or reassurance he sends his word to fortify us.

4. God speaks repeatedly to us over the course of a lifetime. The word of the Lord came to Jeremiah from the time of his call to the time of

the exile, some 40 years (Jeremiah 1:1–3—notice the conjunctions "in", "through" and "down to", indicating continuity). That is not to say God speaks incessantly or without pausing for breath, but to emphasise the joy of an on-going relationship where hearing his voice is not a once in a lifetime experience but a fairly regular occurrence.

God speaks to us through what we see and what we hear. He opens both our eyes and our ears. In this section our focus now will be on how God taught Jeremiah to receive his word through what he saw with his physical eyes and also the eyes of his heart. Later we will consider what it means to have ears to hear.

Reflection

Think about any occasion when the word of the Lord came to you, when you sensed God speaking to you. What happened, and what did you feel God was saying to you?

|13|

SEEING PHYSICALLY

The word of the Lord came to Jeremiah through what he saw right there before him. God asked him a simple question, "What do you see Jeremiah?" He replied with a statement of the obvious: "I see the branch of an almond tree." Nothing too difficult there.

The almond tree is one of the first to flower in the spring, and is known as the "early awake" tree. When it bursts into bud it is as if it has been watching for winter to end and the warmer weather to arrive. There is a play on words here in the Hebrew, for the word for "almond tree" and "watching" sounds very similar. God has also been "watching", waiting for the time when his word will come to pass (v. 12). For so long he had been warning his recalcitrant people that unless they changed their ways judgement would be inevitable. Now the day of accountability has finally arrived. The simple noticing of a tree in blossom became for Jeremiah a way of receiving the word of God, because God spoke to him through what he saw with his natural eyes.

What this implies is that the created world can become for us a means by which God speaks to us. It is as if the whole created order is pregnant with the word of God, if only we have eyes to see. If we walk with our eyes wide open and our hearts alive and alert, we should not be surprised if we hear the still small voice of God in the things we see. God is not locked into sacred buildings or confined to religious services. He inhabits the world he made and his word is everywhere. Neither is his only medium of communication through preaching or reading the Scriptures. These are primary sources through which God speaks, which we must never neglect or devalue, but they are not exclusive channels. God can speak to us wherever we are on planet earth for creation also contains his word.

This thought is summed up in a beautiful quotation attributed to Saint Augustine: "Some people, in order to discover God, read books. But there is a great book: the very appearance of created things. Look above you! Look below you! Note it. Read it. God, whom you want to discover, never wrote that book with ink. Instead He set before your eyes the things that He had made. Can you ask for a louder voice than that? Why, heaven and earth shout to you: 'God made me!'" If we are to be more aware of God it will be because we become more aware of the world around us.

The first way in which God can speak to us through creation is through its grandeur and beauty. Psalm 19 reminds us of the fundamental truth:

"For the heavens declare the glory of God, the skies proclaim the work of his hands.

Day after day they pour forth speech; night after night they display knowledge.

There is no speech or language where their voice is not heard.

Their voice goes out into all the earth, their words to the ends of the world (vv. 1–4)."

Creation speaks eloquently not only of the existence of God but of his character too, and his greatness (Romans 1:20). Whether in the daytime or at night creation is incessantly revealing the glory of God to those who have eyes to see. It speaks a universal language that transcends culture or human tongue, and no place on earth has poor reception. The word is everywhere around us, we need only tune in to its frequency.

Who has not marvelled at a glorious sunset or sunrise, or rejoiced in the warmth of the sun and the beauty of the moon? Whose breath has not been taken by the grandeur of majestic mountains, the power of the oceans, the vastness of a desert? Which of us has not been moved by the intricacy of a flower, intrigued by the colourful variety of birds, fascinated by the ways of the animal kingdom? Have you ever sat beneath a starry sky and not been made to feel that the universe is so great and you are so small? Who doesn't appreciate the seasons, and the rhythm of the tides? What about a cold and frosty morning, the first snow of winter, flowers blooming in spring and the falling of autumn leaves? Don't you love the blueness of the sky and the formations of the clouds? Can you appreciate a cool breeze when it's hot and rainfall when it's been dry? Even storms and hurricanes and earthquakes speak of the magnificence of God—remember Job's experience (Job 38:1–42:6)?

Through it all God is shouting to us, "I'M HERE!" If only we would make the time to slow down, to notice what we are seeing and to savour all that is around us we would know that for ourselves and feel connected to the One who is the Maker of all things. But we insist on living at such a pace we have no time to stand and stare, to drink in the beauty, or to think what it all means, so the word of God drops between our fingers time and again.

God not only speaks to us through the macro view of creation but also through the micro dimension. He is there in the vastness and the grandeur and also in the detail and the minutiae. It seems there are parables of nature just waiting to be discovered, lessons about God wrapped up in his creation. That's how it was for Jeremiah with the almond tree, a message was there for him to read once his eyes were opened. Nature itself can teach us about God and be the medium through which he reveals his truth. What about the caterpillar that becomes a butterfly? Or the grain of wheat that must fall into the earth and die before it bears much fruit? Or the birds that seem to trust in God's provision and never have a care? Or the rainbow that reminds us God will never again flood the earth?

Jesus taught his followers to look, to consider, to pay attention to the world around them so they could recognise not just the hand of God in creation but also his voice (Matthew 6:25–34). It is what we seek to do on an Awareness Walk (see the end of this section), to walk with our eyes fully opened but our hearts attentive to what we are seeing, or rather, to what grabs our attention. The more we practice this simple discipline the more it becomes a way of life for us, so that at any moment in our ordinary day we may suddenly be made aware of that which seems to have been waiting for us to notice. And as we reflect on it we begin to perceive the lesson it contains. Some have called this "contemplative seeing", a way of looking that takes us beyond what is there to the meaning it contains. Artists and photographers know this so well because they have an eye for beauty, but that is not their prerogative alone; it is a possibility for all who will learn to see.

Here is another avenue by which we may find God in the ordinary. It happens when we choose to walk with our eyes wide open, and our hearts receptive to the whisper of God. When we do this we discover as the poet Elizabeth Browning (1806–1861) did, that "Earth's crammed with heaven and every common bush is aflame with God; but only he who sees, takes off his shoes."[10]

༄

Reflection
What comes to mind for you when you think of the glory of creation? Has the detail of the natural world ever caught your attention and become a parable for you?

|14|

SEEING SPIRITUALLY

Elisha the prophet was a wanted man. The king of Aram was incensed because his plans were continually being revealed to Israel by Elisha and he was determined to stop him. Finding he was in the city of Dotham, the king ordered horses and chariots and a strong force of troops to surround the city by night so there was no way of escape. Elisha, however, was not afraid for he knew God was with him.

When his servant woke and saw they were surrounded by hostile forces he was terrified, but Elisha reassured the young man, saying, "Those who are with us are more than those who are with them." Then he prayed, "O lord, open his eyes so that he may see". This time God opened his eyes to see what had been hidden from his sight before, and he saw the horses and chariots of fire that were protecting Elisha (2 Kings 6:8–17). He gained God's perspective on the situation and his fear subsided. The story reminds us that there is more than one way of seeing. Not only can we see things with our physical eyes, but we can also see things spiritually with the eyes of our heart.

God asks Jeremiah a second time, "What do you see (v. 13)?" This time the answer is not something physically before him but an image that has formed in his mind's eye. "I see a boiling pot," he says, "tilting away from the north (v. 13)." This image is a picture of judgement, for disaster will come upon Judah from the north, in the shape of the Babylonians. Once again the word of the Lord has come to Jeremiah only this time it is through a picture he has seen in his mind. Revelation has come through his imagination, but it is not something he has made up. Rather it has been given to him. The word of the Lord has come to him.

This spiritual seeing is something that takes place in our spirit. As human beings made in the image of God we are tripartite beings, composed of our body (the outer person), our soul (the inner person) and our spirit (the deepest part of us). It is in our spirit that we can sense the presence of God and receive the word of God. The human spirit is the location of our faculties of intuition and perception, both of which are integral to this ability to see spiritually. When the apostle Paul prayed for the Ephesian believers he asked that God will give them the Spirit of wisdom and revelation so that they may know God more deeply. Then he said, "I pray also that the eyes of your heart may be enlightened in order that you may know the hope to which he has called you, the riches of his glorious inheritance in the saints, and his incomparably great power for us who believe (Ephesians 1:18–19)." The apostle recognised that the way we grasp spiritual truth is by revelation. We are taught by the Holy Spirit who opens the eyes of our hearts (our spirit) so that we can see. When this happens, our minds are enlightened too and we can understand. Our minds are flooded with the light of the knowledge of the glory of God (2 Corinthians 4:6).

This is what John Stott calls the Holy Spirit's "ministry of illumination".[11] The Spirit takes the truth of God and makes it real to us (John 16:13). As we are reading the Bible or listening to its truth being taught, we begin to grasp its meaning for ourselves. It is as if the penny drops, and we exclaim, "Oh, now I see!" The Holy Spirit has opened the eyes of our hearts and our mind has been enlightened with understanding and insight. It is why the Psalmist prayed, "Open my eyes that I may see wonderful things in your law (Psalm 119:18)."

There are three main ways in which we can see spiritually. The first is through mental pictures as in this instance. God used Jeremiah's imagination to create in his mind the picture of a boiling pot spilling over and then gave him the understanding of what it meant. This is often how God speaks to people in times of worship or prayer. They receive a mental picture and a sense that God is speaking to them (or others) through what they see. How do we know that this is not simply our own imagination or make believe? That is always a danger, but the genuine can be discerned because it *comes to us* without any effort on our part. It is *given*, usually when we are focused on God and not at all looking for it. The meaning, too, is usually clear, and confirmed by others. That which is valid will always be in line with the teaching of Scripture and will bring encouragement and hope.

A second way of seeing is through dreams. We have seen already that God spoke to Jacob through a dream, and dreams are common both in the Old and New Testaments. Think for example of how God spoke to Joseph in the Birth Stories (Matthew 1:20, 2:13, 19 and 22). Most of our dreams will not be messages from God but occasionally they may be. Dreams we know can reveal what is in our subconscious and they may make us aware of our hidden fears or desires. They can also be a way by which God speaks to us. When this happens, the dream is usually clear and memorable, and the meaning comes with it. They bring their own authentication so that we know God has spoken to us, but they also stand the scrutiny of others who can confirm whether they are of God or not. They don't fade with time, and most importantly, are seen to come true.

In the course of my life I have had perhaps three dreams like this. One occurred when I was at a time of transition and taking a step of faith into a new ministry without salary. In the dream I was holding my hand out and a little sparrow came flying towards me and rested in my palm. I assumed that it had come so that I could feed it, but then it flew away again. When it returned it brought with it a piece of bread and placed it in my hand, as if to feed me. When I woke I felt God say to me, "I will supply all your needs", and this has been amazingly true. For the last 12 years God has provided for us abundantly and in surprising ways, and we have never been in need.

The third aspect of seeing is through visions. A vision is like a dream except we are awake, and again there are many examples in Scripture. Take, for example, Peter's vision of the sheet full of all kinds of creatures being lowered from heaven. It occurred in the context of prayer, and with a message from God that Peter should not call anything impure that God had made clean. This vision, followed as it was by the visit of Cornelius, would have a remarkable impact in helping the early believers realise that the Gentiles too were to be welcomed into the kingdom (Acts 10:9–23). Likewise the apostle Paul was guided on his missionary journey by a vision of a man from Macedonia asking for help. From this the apostle concluded that this was God's call and he and his team moved on to Philippi as a result (Acts 16:6–10). It seems clear that God occasionally uses visions to grab our attention, in particular when it comes to pioneering new inroads for the gospel. Again they bring their own sense of authenticity that can be affirmed by others but is best seen in the positive outcome that follows.

If we want to grow in this area of spiritual seeing, we must pray along with the apostle Paul that God will daily open our eyes and grant us the Spirit of wisdom and revelation. This privilege is not for some elite group of super-spiritual people but for all God's children who aspire to receive his word. Then we must trust that what we receive is indeed from God, and prayerfully decide how we might share what has been given to us. It may be something that is for our own sake, so we keep it in our hearts. It may be that it is for another person, or for the whole church, in which case when the time is right, and with humility, we can share what we have been given for their consideration and discernment.

✻

Reflection

How aware are you of the deeper, spiritual dimension to life? Make sure that your perspective is not limited to the material world around you, but includes also the invisible, spiritual realm of which the Bible speaks.

|15|

EYES TO SEE ?

A friend of mine has been blind from birth and has never seen anything with her physical eyes, and yet her insight into spiritual truth is remarkable. She can see clearly with the eyes of her heart, and God has used her greatly to bring encouragement and healing to others through her worship songs. Some people by contrast have tip-top physical vision but remain spiritually blind.

This danger is one that the prophets continually spoke about. Isaiah warned the people of his day, "Be ever hearing but never understanding; be ever seeing, but never perceiving (Isaiah 6:9)." He counselled them against becoming spiritually calloused, hard of hearing and lacking in sight. John interprets the refusal to believe in Jesus by those who saw the miraculous signs of Jesus as fulfilling Isaiah's words (John 12:37–41). Likewise, Paul attributed the stubborn rejection of his message by some of the Jews in Rome to the same condition—they were spiritually blind—and quoted the same words (Acts 28:23–28).

None of us is immune to this danger but there is a remedy for spiritual eye disease. To the church at Laodicea, characterised as being lukewarm and self-satisfied, the message from the Spirit is to buy from him "salve to put on your eyes so that you may see (Revelation 4:18)." This healing comes about through genuine repentance. When we humble ourselves before God, and are willing to recognise our true condition, our spiritual eyesight is restored. Sound vision is not something we should take for granted. How then can we make sure our sight remains good?

Primarily we should make sure our "lens" is clean. The eye gate is one of the main avenues by which our souls interact with the world, and yet there is so much visual material out there that is unhelpful to spiritual growth. Jesus said, "Blessed are the pure in heart, for they will see God (Matthew 5:8)." We keep our hearts pure by guarding what we feast our eyes upon. When our hearts are pure we will have clearer spiritual vision. The lust of the eyes is one of the main avenues that sin finds a place in our hearts (1 John 1:16). The focus may be on material things that we covet, computer games that we play with their vicarious violence, or internet pornography that we watch. Our spiritual well-being can be adversely affected by TV programmes or films that we watch which portray a lifestyle and values that are contrary to those of God's kingdom. All of these deaden our appetite for God, rob us of spiritual vitality, and dirty the lens of our hearts so that we can no longer see spiritually. Pornography in itself is now a world-wide epidemic across all ages and genders. Its tentacles spread everywhere and affects the most noble of people. We must do what Job did and make a covenant with our eyes (Job 31:1), find an accountability partner and pray for God to release you from its powerful grip.

Something else that will help us seek clearly is the maintenance of a child-like attitude of dependency and trust in God. In one of his lesser known prayers Jesus thanked God that spiritual insight was hidden from the "wise and learned" and revealed to "little children" (Matthew 11:25–26). This does not mean that we should despise learning or education but that we should not depend on them as the basis for our relationship with God. Knowledge has a way of puffing up the ego, whereas those who are childlike remain humble because they are aware of how much they don't know. This humility of heart makes them teachable, an essential requirement of all who would know God more deeply: "This is the one I esteem: he who is humble and contrite in spirit, and trembles at my word (Isaiah 66:2)."

Alongside this we must maintain a servant's heart towards God. The writer of Psalm 123 begins by fixing his eyes on God: "I lift up my eyes, to you whose throne is in heaven (v. 1)." This recognition of who God is, and of our place before him, keeps us humble and grounded and reminds us that we are called to be servants of God. This disposition then becomes ingrained in how we approach God: "As the eyes of slaves look to the hand of their master, as the eyes of a maid look to the hand of her mistress, so our eyes look to the Lord our God, till he shows us his mercy (v. 2)." When our basic desire is to please God and to do his will then we can be sure that we will see well because we will be more attentive to his direction and attuned to his desires. This will make it easier for us to see with the eyes of our heart.

Everyone knows the value of having a regular check-up at the optician's so that any developing problems can be dealt with as early as possible. It is the same spiritually. Why not give yourself a simple eye test by asking these questions: Am I looking at the right things? Am I still humble and teachable? Is my attitude that of a servant who is eager to please?

Reflection

How would you evaluate the clarity with which you are seeing things spiritually? How are you taking care of your eyes?

SPIRITUAL PRACTICE

Awareness Walk

A helpful way to notice God in creation is to go for an awareness walk. Jesus told his disciples to be aware of the world around them because, as we have seen, it speaks of God (Psalm 19:1–6). He told them to look at the birds of the air, and to see how the lilies grow because by observing the natural world we can encounter God (Matthew 6:26, 28). This is something we can do intentionally, as a spiritual discipline, and after a while it will become second nature to us. Wherever we are we will start to notice God.

Go for a very leisurely walk outside—or just sit quietly observing all that is around you. Prayerfully ask God to open your eyes to all that is before you, then notice what you notice. Be alert to those things which grab your attention, which "accidentally" come across your path. Recognise that God is in such happenings. Use your five senses (to see, hear, taste, touch, smell) to engage with the world which God the Creator has made. What you see is not by accident or chance. God drew your attention to it. Ponder its meaning and significance.

Now look …

> Imagine God saying to you, "What do you **see**?" A bird, a beetle, a worm, a spider's web?

> Look at the grasses—many different kinds … **touch** them … look carefully at them ….

> Look at the flowers—touch them gently so that you do not harm them …. Look at the stamens, sepals, the leaves, the blossoms … **smell** their fragrance.

Look at the trees—so many different varieties, shades of green, different leaves, bark, fruit … notice their form, shape and size.

Now listen …

No doubt you may hear cars but what else can you **hear**? A bird? The rustling of leaves? The chirrup of an insect? What do the noises say to you?

Perhaps there is something you can **taste**?

Now look at the larger scene …

The great trees … the patterns in the clouds … the colours of the sky … How does it speak of God?

What is it saying to you? Can you recognise some of the parables in nature that speak to you, today, in your present situation?

Remember: all this was made by God … worship Him who made it all with such beauty, detail, individuality and order.

Perhaps collect a few things which will not spoil the garden or the countryside to take back to make a small display.

Finally, why not journal about your findings? By doing this you can reserve the memory of what you experienced.

Why not take a camera with you or use your smart phone to capture what you see—photography can be a very contemplative way of seeing the world. Take pictures that say something, that communicate a simple message, which can illustrate a Bible truth or Scripture verse. Post your pictures on social media for others to enjoy. Perhaps make a scrap book of things you have seen as a reminder for later. ✿

Part 4

Samuel, and the Posture of Listening

¹ The boy Samuel ministered before the Lord under Eli. In those days the word of the Lord was rare; there were not many visions.

² One night Eli, whose eyes were becoming so weak that he could barely see, was lying down in his usual place. ³ The lamp of God had not yet gone out, and Samuel was lying down in the house of the Lord, where the ark of God was. ⁴ Then the Lord called Samuel.

Samuel answered, "Here I am." ⁵ And he ran to Eli and said, "Here I am; you called me."

But Eli said, "I did not call; go back and lie down." So he went and lay down.

⁶ Again the Lord called, "Samuel!" And Samuel got up and went to Eli and said, "Here I am; you called me."

"My son," Eli said, "I did not call; go back and lie down."

⁷ Now Samuel did not yet know the Lord: The word of the Lord had not yet been revealed to him.

⁸ A third time the Lord called, "Samuel!" And Samuel got up and went to Eli and said, "Here I am; you called me."

Then Eli realized that the Lord was calling the boy. ⁹ So Eli told Samuel, "Go and lie down, and if he calls you, say, 'Speak, Lord, for your servant is listening.'" So Samuel went and lay down in his place.

¹⁰ The Lord came and stood there, calling as at the other times, "Samuel! Samuel!"

Then Samuel said, "Speak, for your servant is listening."

|16|

SAMUEL'S STORY

If ever we could say with certainty that a person had been chosen by God for a specific work then that person must be Samuel. The story of his birth and upbringing bears all the hallmarks of God's providence, demonstrating the meticulous way in which God prepares and shapes those through whom he wants to accomplish his purposes.

Samuel's parents were Elkanah and Hannah, a couple deeply devoted to God and sincere in their faith, who actively walked with God at a time when many in Israel were lukewarm. They lived, however, with a deep sorrow in their hearts that is common to many couples today—they were childless. For Hannah this was a devastating blow that wounded her painfully, but despite the temptation to feel bitter or angry with God she allowed her trouble to draw her closer to him.

Somewhat in desperation she went to the tabernacle in Shiloh and poured her soul out to God, weeping and praying before him. There she cried to God for help, promising that if God gave her a son she would offer him back to the Lord for his service (1 Samuel 1:10–11). When Eli the priest affirmed her request she returned home lighter in heart, and with renewed hope. Sometime later she conceived and gave birth to a boy.

Recognising the miraculous aspect of the birth, she called her son Samuel which means either "heard of God" or "asked of God". Once the child was weaned (perhaps about three years old) she took him back to Shiloh and, as she had promised, in gratitude gave him back to the Lord and to the care of Eli (1 Samuel 1:27–28). This would have been a heart-wrenching decision for any mother, but one which God blessed for the boy went from strength to strength as he served daily in the tabernacle.

The Bible story highlights the spiritual growth that Samuel experienced even as a child and shows how firmly God's hand was upon him from his earliest years. We are told that he ministered before the Lord under Eli (1 Samuel 2:11). The famous commentator Matthew Henry suggests that the boy Samuel "could light a candle, or hold a dish, or run an errand, or shut a door; and because he did this with a pious disposition of mind it is called *ministering to the Lord.*" (his italics)[12] Whatever his duties involved, it seems clear that from a very young age he learned to serve and to see the performance of these menial tasks as a way of pleasing God. Here is a reminder to us all that we can fulfil our daily duties, however mundane, with an eye to pleasing God. God is to be found in the ordinary.

At the same time, Samuel was growing spiritually and as the years passed by and he observed the rituals of the tabernacle and began to understand their meaning, he began to mature spiritually as well: "the boy Samuel grew up in the presence of the Lord (1 Samuel 2:21)." His progress was noted by others too, and even as he grew taller physically his spiritual development and humility marked him out as being a youngster particularly blessed by God: "And the boy Samuel continued to grow in stature and favour with the Lord and with people (1 Samuel 2:26)." He learned to be attentive to Eli, and attentive to God. In this way God prepared him for the significant role he would have one day in the life of Israel.

It is often said that Samuel was the last of the judges and the first of the prophets. There was certainly something of the charismatic leader about him (1 Samuel 7:2–13 and 15–17), but it is as a prophet, someone attuned to the voice of God, that he is mostly remembered (1 Samuel 3:19–21). Such a ministry did not come to him without a period of struggle, and at first he did not recognise God's voice so easily—"Now Samuel did not yet know the Lord: The word of the Lord had not yet been revealed to him (1 Samuel 3:7)."

What this teaches us is that all of us have to learn how to hear the voice of God and to recognise when he is speaking to us. Samuel learned to do this as a child, a reminder that young people with a heart for God are able to enter into a living relationship with him and to recognise his voice at an early age. Perhaps a child-like heart is a helpful attitude to cultivate as we seek to know God more deeply. After all, Jesus said that many things are hidden from the wise and learned but revealed to little children (Matthew 11:25–26). Maybe we will need to become more humble, more trusting, and a little less sophisticated as we pursue our desire to be more aware of God in our everyday lives. There is no shame in admitting that we have still a lot to learn or that we are unschooled in hearing God's voice. What matters most is that we have the longing to be more attentive.

Reflection

Hearing the voice of God is something that we all have to learn how to do, and that takes time, but if a young boy like Samuel could recognise God's voice, so can you.

|17|

EARS TO HEAR

Samuel grew up at a time in Israel when the spiritual life of God's people was at a low ebb, and as a result the word of the Lord was rare. It was a period similar to the time of the prophet Amos when there was a famine of hearing the word of the Lord (Amos 8:11). All that was soon to change, however, for God was about to speak again and had prepared Samuel for the task of receiving his word.

The writer to the Hebrews reminds us at the start of his epistle that God is a God who speaks, and does so in a variety of ways. Looking back to the days of the Old Testament he says, "In the past God spoke to our forefathers through the prophets at many times and in various ways (Hebrews 1:1)." Here we are reminded that God loves to communicate with his people. He desires that they know what is on his heart, what his purposes are, and how he wants them to respond. Samuel was the first of a line of prophets who throughout the history of Israel brought God's word to his people.

God communicated to his prophets by many different means: by dreams, and visions, with an audible voice, through circumstances and natural events, in angelic visitations and even on one occasion

shows God's patience

through a donkey (Numbers 22:28)! What this shows is the intensity of God's desire to speak to his people. The word of God came primarily to those with a prophetic calling (like Isaiah, Jeremiah and so on) but also to other godly people like Abraham, Moses and David. At the same time, there seems to have been an understanding that all of Israel was capable of recognising when God was speaking to the nation, and that they had a responsibility to hear and obey: "Today, if you hear his voice, do not harden your hearts" was the call (Psalm 95:7–8, Hebrews 4:7–8 and 15).

What Hebrews goes on to make clear is that a new dispensation has now come into being that far exceeds that of the Old Testament, which was by nature partial and incomplete: "in these last days he has spoken to us by his Son" the writer boldly declares (Hebrews 1:2). The thrust of this great epistle is that Jesus through his death and resurrection has now ushered in a New Covenant and a much more effective way of relating to God. All that the Old Testament hinted at and suggested now finds its completion and fulfilment in Christ who has opened for us a new and living way by which we may approach God with a boldness and confidence never known before. Everything about this new order of things is both better and superior to what had gone before (Hebrews 1:4, 7:19 and 22, 8:6, 9:23).

The benefits of this New Covenant, first prophesied by Jeremiah, are outlined for us in Hebrews 8:7–13. As well as bringing to us the complete forgiveness of our sins (v. 12), what is also made possible is that every believer will now be able to know the Lord personally rather than in a second-hand sort of way: "they will all know me, from the least of them to the greatest (v. 11)." Each will be able to say, "God is *my* God." The kind of intimate relationship that under the old system was limited to a few is now the privilege of all, regardless of status, race, ability or gender. It is now possible for each believer, young and old, to know and relate to God for themselves.

How does this happen? By the miracle that we call regeneration, whereby the Holy Spirit begins to impart to us the personal knowledge of God. This is what God says will happen: "I will put my laws in their minds and write them on their hearts, I will be their God and they will be my people (v. 10)." Here is an amazing promise that every believer should take note of, and around which the whole of our on-going relationship with God depends. The Holy Spirit will renew our minds and plant within our hearts the desire to please God and walk in his ways. Without this interior work it would be impossible for us to live the Christian life; because of it we can now grow in our relationship with God, and—importantly for what we are talking about here—we can now hear God speaking to us.

This reality, that God's new Covenant people will hear his voice, is something that Jesus spoke about to his disciples. In John 10 Jesus refers to himself as the good shepherd, while his disciples are his sheep, and the characteristic of his sheep is that they listen to his shepherd's voice (v2). He says, "When he has brought out all his own, he goes on ahead of them, and his sheep follow him *because they know his voice* (vv. 3–4, my italics)." He then continues to talk about laying down his life for his sheep, and also of bringing other sheep to him who are not yet in the fold, saying the same thing about them: "*They too will listen to my voice*, and there shall be one flock and one shepherd (v. 16, my italics)." And if this double confirmation is not enough to convince us, he follows it with a third statement of this great foundational truth: "*My sheep listen to my voice*: I know them, and they follow me (v. 27, my italics)." Clearly then Jesus believed that his followers would be able to hear and recognise his voice for themselves.

One of the favourite sayings of Jesus seems to have been this: "he who has ears, let him hear", used on at least four different occasions and repeated throughout the gospels (Matthew 11:15, 13:9, 13:43, Luke 14:35). Whenever he was teaching his followers Jesus expected that they would be able not only to hear him audibly, but also spiritually, to recognise that God the Father was speaking through him: "These words you hear are not my own; they belong to the Father who sent me (John 14:24)." He constantly challenged his disciples to sharpen their listening skills and to be more attentive to what God was doing and saying. After the two feeding miracles, of five thousand people and then four thousand, the disciples appear not to have grasped the significance of what had happened. He rebuked them with these words: "Do you have eyes but fail to see, and ears but fail to hear (Mark 8:18)?" Not only can we hear God speak to us, but we have a responsibility to pay attention and not miss what he may be saying.

Over the years that I have conducted retreats and taught about intimacy with God I have been saddened by the number of people, genuinely committed believers, who have shared with me, somewhat downcast, that they never hear God speak to them. I feel real sympathy for such people, and I do not want to pass judgement on them, but I believe it does not have to be that way. Perhaps for many God does speak to them but they fail to hear his voice because they are too distracted by their busyness. In their frantic lives they miss the moment. Others may be so down on themselves that they have no expectation that God would address them anyway. They feel unworthy of being spoken to by God, undeserving of such a privilege. A good number will never have been taught how to recognise God's voice. They are like Samuel, still untrained in the ways of God. We might say the word of the Lord has not yet been revealed to them. Some churches are not good at helping their members develop their spiritual hearing, so many believers still lack confidence in recognising God's voice for themselves.

Whatever the reason, it is a sad state of affairs, and I want to encourage such people to remember that the ability to hear God's voice is part of our birthright as God's people and that we can expect God to communicate with us. Yes, we need to learn how to attend to both his presence and his voice, but it should be our expectation that God will speak, and we will hear. This is not beyond any of us and is not something simply for the spiritual elite. If a boy like Samuel could recognise and respond to the overture of God, so can we, his born-again children of the New Covenant. We also have ears to hear.

⚘

Reflection

Thank God for the gift of hearing and that you also have "ears to hear" what God is saying. Believe Jesus when he says that you too can hear his voice.

|18|

THE POSTURE OF LISTENING

The priest Eli may have been slow to recognise that it was God who was calling the boy, but he got there in the end, and his word of advice was sound: "Go and lie down, and if he calls you, say, 'Speak Lord, for your servant is listening (1 Samuel 3:9).'" Thus Samuel returned to his bed, put out the light and went to sleep.

We hear God's voice best when we are most relaxed. Eli wisely does not tell the boy to stay awake all night, pacing up and down in case he should miss the moment of God's call. No, he tells him to lie down and relax because God is well able to make himself heard. In my experience people who get too intense about hearing God's voice seldom do so. This self-preoccupation becomes a barrier to spiritual receptivity. I always encourage people who come on retreat—especially those who come because they have an important reason for hearing God's voice—to remember that the posture of listening begins by being relaxed. We must try not to get too worked up about it. God will speak when he is ready and he will make sure we hear.

The quietness of the tabernacle at night proved to be a helpful setting for Samuel's first experience of hearing God. All the visitors were gone and everything was stilled, and as Samuel rested he too was quiet. There seems to be a direct correlation between stillness and silence and our ability to hear God. The Psalmist said, "Be still, and know that I am God (Psalm 46:10)", which suggests there are some things about God that can only be known in the stillness. This is why many people take time out of their busy schedules for retreat and consciously seek solitude and silence. They know they are more likely to meet with God when their souls are still and at rest. It also explains why God often chooses the night hours to speak to us. When everything around us is still, and we are stilled within, we seem to be more receptive to God. This has certainly often been my experience, and it appears to have been that of the servant described by Isaiah in the Servant Songs: "He wakens me morning by morning, wakens my ear to listen like one being taught (Isaiah 50:4)."[13]

A third factor in Samuel's preparation for receiving God's word is seen in the attitude of his heart. His approach to God is that of a servant to his master, one of submission and willingness to obey: "Speak, for your servant is listening." This readiness to do God's will whatever it may be seems to heighten our ability to recognise when God is speaking to us. If there is a struggle within us over whether or not to obey God we are more likely to become confused and hesitant when it comes to discerning his will. Jesus hinted at this when speaking to a group of sceptical Jews: "If anyone chooses to do God's will, he will find out whether my teaching comes from God or whether I speak on my own (John 7:16)." The more committed we are to doing God's will, and the more sincerely we desire to obey him, then the more likely we are to hear his voice when he speaks.

What we see here then is that the posture of listening involves being relaxed, being still and being willing to do whatever God asks of us. When these things are in place our ability to discern God's voice will be greatly enhanced. Yet we have to admit that hearing his voice is not always straightforward, no matter how experienced we may be. Sometimes God seems strangely silent, and sometimes our hearing seems, for no apparent reason, to be somewhat dulled. This listening to God is not a process in which we are in control. We cannot conjure up a word from God at will. God speaks when he is ready, and we must learn to wait patiently and humbly for his timing.

The promise, however, remains clear: "Whether you turn to the right or the left, your ears will hear a voice behind you, saying 'This is the way; walk in it (Isaiah 30:21).'" Here is an assurance of divine guidance, of providential care, of being led in the right way. God does not want his people to be confused or to get lost, so he speaks to them when the time is right, but the voice comes from behind them. It is like when a traveller standing at a crossroads, uncertain which way to take, is addressed by a fellow traveller coming up from *behind* him. This person knows the road better and is able to point the person in the right direction. Alternatively, we may think of it as the way some shepherds guide their sheep from behind, calling to them when they are about to wander from the path. Either way, the message is that when we are at a junction in life we will find the direction we need.

The voice in question is of course the voice of God, or as we may equally say, the voice of the Holy Spirit, who is our Comforter, Teacher and Guide (John 14:16, 26 and 16:13). This is seldom an audible, external voice, but usually an internal, quiet voice that we hear in our spirit. We have already said in Chapter 13 that as human beings we are made in the image of God, and are tripartite beings, composed of our body (the outer person), our soul (the inner person) and our spirit (the deepest part of us). It is in our spirit that we can sense the presence of God and receive the word of God. There we thought about the eyes of our hearts being opened so that we can see spiritually. Here we are thinking about how our "ears" can be opened to hear the voice of God, what is often called "the still, small voice of God".

This well-known expression comes from the story of Elijah in 1 Kings 19. Tired and exhausted after his contest with the priests and Baal on Mount Carmel, and terrified by the subsequent threats of Queen Jezebel, Elijah flees for his life to a cave on mount Horeb. There God comes to reassure and strengthen him, speaking to him not through the noise of the wind, the earthquake or the fire, but surprisingly through a "gentle whisper (v. 12)"—a still, small voice, or as it may also be translated, "a sound of sheer silence".

This gentle whisper that we hear is the Holy Spirit speaking to us. We have the ability to recognise it and to respond to his voice, and the more we do so the more skilled we become in recognising it and distinguishing it from other voices. The apostle Paul says in Romans 8:16, "The Spirit himself bears witness with our spirit that we are God's children." The sense of assurance we feel in our hearts when we come to faith in Christ is probably the first time we hear that voice. He tells us that we belong to God, that we have been forgiven, that we are accepted, and he does so not in an audible way but in the whisper of love—a quiet knowing deep within that we are now God's children. The inner witness of the Spirit is one of the main ways by which we come to hear the voice of God and as we mature in our faith we will learn to "sense" his presence and his will in other ways too.

There is more to the work of the Spirit in us though. The Spirit also occasionally speaks words to us, words that we hear in our innermost being. We see this ministry at work in the life of Philip the evangelist. He had been led by God to go down from Jerusalem to Gaza, and as he did so he met an Ethiopian eunuch travelling southwards in his chariot. Then God spoke to him with that inner voice. "The Spirit told Philip, 'Go to that chariot and stay near it (Acts 8:29).'" It was not an audible voice, but an internal one, a feeling or an impression that he recognised came from God and which he obeyed. It was a little nudge from behind, pointing him in the right direction. He discovered that the Ethiopian was already reading the Scriptures and wanted help in understanding the passage before him. Philip was delighted to help, and told him the good news of Jesus, after which the man was baptised.

All this happened because Philip recognised the prompting of the Holy Spirit and responded in faith and obedience. It reminds us of the exciting adventure that awaits us as we too learn to discern the voice of God and respond to his leading. Through the witness of the Spirit and the words of the Spirit we are drawn into a living relationship with the God who continues to speak to his people today. What matters is that we learn to develop, and maintain, a posture of listening.

𝔏

Reflection

Why not take a moment or two to be still and quiet.
Once you are relaxed and undisturbed, listen for the voice of God
in the quietness of your heart. What do you hear?

|19|

INCLINE YOUR EAR

What began for Samuel as a first encounter with God in the tabernacle that night became for him a pattern and a way of life. He grew up to become a man skilled in hearing the voice of God and his effectiveness was recognised by others: "And all Israel . . . recognised that Samuel was attested as a prophet of the Lord (1 Samuel 3:20)." What is more, God continued to reveal himself and his word to Samuel, and made sure that his words came to pass (1 Samuel 3:19–21). We may not have the prophetic ministry that Samuel had but under the terms of the New Covenant we too can enjoy a lifetime of communicating with God.

I became a Christian as a teenager and consider myself fortunate that from those early years I was encouraged to spend time daily in reading the Bible and in praying. This regular diet of Scripture (through which God speaks to us) and prayer (through which we speak to him) has formed the backdrop to my life for over 50 years and has perhaps been the most significant single factor in my spiritual formation. Like many others, I have lived with an on-going conversation with God. It is not that I have followed this simple discipline rigidly or consistently all the time. There have been periods when I have been neglectful and many days when I considered myself to be too busy, yet this simple practice has always been part of the rhythm of my life, and it has served me well. I still wish I had spent more time in God's word, yet I am thankful for the reservoir of Scriptural insight that has built up in my life over the decades even when my application has been somewhat patchy.

I regard the Bible as God's inspired word, brought into being by the Holy Spirit (2 Timothy 3:14–17). Like the Psalmist, I love the Scriptures for they have indeed been a light to my path and a lamp for my feet (Psalm 119:105). I expect therefore that when I read them, God will speak to me because the Bible is God's revealed word to us. It has a power of its own, and when we read the Bible with the help of the Holy Spirit it can reach deep into our hearts in a way that leaves us in no doubt that it is God who is speaking. As Hebrews 4:12–13 says, "For the word of God is living and active. Sharper than any double-edged sword, it penetrates even to dividing soul and spirit, joints and marrow; it judges the thoughts and attitudes of the heart." Far from being merely a dull history book the Bible breathes with the very presence of a living God who speaks with relevance in the 21st Century.

Often, when I am reading Scripture nothing special seems to be happening, but God is still speaking. I am hearing his word. On those days I remind myself that by allowing the word of God to enter my mind and heart I am in fact allowing the word of Christ to dwell in me richly (Colossians 3:16), renewing my mind and creating a storehouse of Bible knowledge that the Spirit can later call upon to bring to my remembrance. Occasionally, though, there are moments when the words seem to jump off the page to gain my attention; words of encouragement, challenge or even rebuke. Then I know that God is speaking to me directly and that I must heed and respond to what he is saying. This is the *work of the Spirit*, and in my experience he is very effective at taking the things of God and making them real to us (John 16:14).

When we encounter God in Scripture in this way and respond to him in prayer, we establish an on-going dialogue, something essential in any healthy relationship. He speaks to us and we speak back to him in prayer, sharing our thoughts and longings with him —our need for strength and grace to do his will, faith to believe his promises, wisdom to know how to apply his truth to our daily lives, and so on. We are not talking here about some massively supernatural event. No, this is the bread and butter of Christian discipleship, a simple discipline that all can follow, and through which God speaks to us in the ordinariness of our days.

On to this foundation I want to add a second layer of communication, one that we have already mentioned, the *witness of the Spirit* deep in our hearts. We considered in the last chapter the way in which the Spirit brings assurance to our hearts but there are other ways in which we can experience this "sense" of God speaking to us. It does not come in either audible or interior words particularly, but more as an impression that cannot be ignored. Sometimes it will be a sense of conviction that we should either do something or, alternatively, not do something. This may be because we sense certain actions may be right or wrong before God, or simply that one action may be in line with God's will while another may be against it. Thus, Paul and his friends were restrained from moving into Asia and Bythinia, but constrained to move into Macedonia (Acts 16:6–10).

Sometimes this inner witness can be experienced as the faintest of whispers or the gentlest of *nudges*—an impression, say, that we should call a certain person, pray for someone, make a gift, write a note or take a particular course of action. We could give many such examples. It may or may not be God speaking to us, but often it is, although we may only realise this afterwards. I was asked by a friend to lead a Bible study for his home group. I was not sure what to share with them, but into my mind came Psalm 84. I had a sense of peace about it, so went to the group and shared as I had been asked. The study went well so I felt it had been the right word, but afterwards I felt even more strongly that I should use the same passage in some other situations, which again I did to good effect. Was God speaking to me when Psalm 84 popped into my mind? I believe so, and I am glad that I registered this faintest of whispers. Be prepared for God to prompt you in this way as well, and have the courage when he does to take a risk and go with what your spirit is telling you.

We can also add a third layer to the way in which God may speak to us and that is through the _words of the Spirit_. Sometimes words come to us directly from the Spirit himself and, while very occasionally these may be audible, more usually we hear them in our spirit. These arise unbidden, and bring with them a definite sense that this is not our own thinking, it is God speaking. We saw already the example of Philip the evangelist, but I want to remind you of something that happened to the apostle Paul which he described for us in 2 Corinthians 12:7–10. He was troubled by a painful "thorn in the flesh" and Satan was using it to disturb and distract him from his mission. Paul naturally took it to God in prayer, asking for its removal, but after three prolonged seasons of prayer nothing had changed. Then it was that the apostle, exhausted and distressed, heard the still, small voice: "My grace is sufficient for you, for my power is made perfect in weakness (2 Corinthians 12:9)." These are famous words that have strengthened many down the centuries, but it is the words that come before this great statement that I want to highlight to you. Paul simply says, "But _he_ said to _me_ (v. 9, my italics)." Here is a wonderfully clear example of how the Spirit speaks personal words into our hearts when we most need them, words of assurance or guidance, words of healing or hope.

Such moments are not happening all the time, and may even be quite rare, but when they come they are memorable and the truth stays with us. I will share just one example from my own experience. When I was a church leader some years ago, we were going through a very discouraging period. I was out walking one day on a wet, cloudy, overcast day which exactly suited my mood. As I walked, the words of a hymn came into my mind, unbidden and yet with a certain weightiness: "Bright skies will soon be o'er me, where the dark clouds have been." You may recognise them from the famous hymn, "In Heavenly Love Abiding", by Anna Waring (1823–1910). Immediately I felt my mood lift as the words brought a glimmer of hope to my soul. As I walked on, I turned a corner and there before me stood two enormous oaks trees, well known locally because of their size and age. It was November and they were completely bare of leaves, shorn of all sign of life. They looked very sad, but as I pondered them a voice within me seemed to say, "They are bare now, but they will not always be", and I knew that God had spoken to me about the future of the church. Just as spring would bring new life to the oaks, so in due course new life would come to our congregation, and it did.

What I am suggesting here is that there are three different levels at which God speaks to us. The most common level is through Scripture as the Holy Spirit takes the word of God and makes it real to us. The second, somewhat less frequent, level is when the Holy Spirit bears witness with our spirit regarding God's will for us and gives us a "sense" of what he wants us to do. It may come as a moment of assurance, of conviction, of leading, but however it comes we know intuitively it is God speaking to us, albeit without words and more through an internal impression. Then the third, and most infrequent, level is when the Holy Spirit speaks words to us directly. This doesn't happen all that often, and we can never tell when it will happen, but when it does it brings its own self-authentication, and the words stay with us.

A living relationship with God will involve communication and dialogue on all three levels. That does not mean that God is a chatterbox who always has something to say. Sometimes there are periods of quiet, of companionable silence, which are normal in any relationship. But there is always enough speaking to keep the relationship alive and to make for a degree of intimacy. This has been my experience and that of countless others. I believe it is what God desires for each of his children. If we incline our ear, in due course he will speak.

※

Reflection

Think about occasions when God has spoken to you through Scripture. What was the setting, and what did God say?

|20|

Is That You God?

Both Eli and Samuel had difficulty in recognising the voice of God. Samuel thought it was Eli calling him, and Eli probably thought it was the boy's imagination. Eventually, on the third time, Eli began to realise it may well be God calling the boy. What this shows is that it is not always easy to determine if it is God speaking to us or not. We need discernment.

God has many means by which he speaks to us. Primarily, he speaks through the Scriptures and the inner witness of the Holy Spirit, but also in many other more ordinary ways. We can encounter his voice while watching a film, reading a book, listening to music, sharing in conversation, looking at art, taking part in exercise, receiving the sacraments, being in church … you can probably add to the list. Once we are aware that God speaks to his people, and that we can hear his voice, there is no shortage of ways by which we can receive his words. The question is, are we hearing correctly, and is it God who is speaking to us?

We have probably all met people who claim to have heard from God when it seems obvious to everyone else that they haven't! God has been made responsible, by well-meaning individuals, for many things he never sanctioned. Some people seem privy to a direct line to heaven and appear to be in constant touch with God about all manner of inconsequential issues while others are sure God has grandiose plans for them. We must all have the humility to recognise that we each have the capacity to deceive ourselves, to let our imaginations run away with us and to turn our wishes into God's will. We also know that we can be deceived by the devil. As writer Richard Peace notes, "The great danger when it comes to 'hearing God' is attribution—describing our inner wants or needs as "from God" when they are just wishful thinking or unconscious narcissism."[14] So how can we protect ourselves from being led astray, and how can we know that it really is God who is speaking to us?

If we are to avoid self-deception, it is important that we have a good understanding of ourselves and that we know our own hearts. If we are prone to grandiose ideas or to fantasising, we are vulnerable to deception. If we are overly ambitious or suffer from an inflated ego, we may well be carried away into flights of fancy. The apostle Paul encourages healthy self-examination: "If anyone thinks he is something when he is nothing, he deceives himself. Each one should test his own actions (Galatians 6:4)." We must rather develop a deep humility of heart and a genuine submission to God that is concerned to do his will, not our own. This will require us to be brutally honest with ourselves about our motivations and desires, and be willing to receive constructive feedback from others who know us well. As the Psalmist said, "He guides the humble in what is right and teaches them his way (Psalm 25:9)."

Furthermore, we must pay careful attention to our own walk with God. We discern God's voice best when we are in a place of spiritual health. When we are rooted in a local church congregation, regularly practising the spiritual disciplines, nurturing mature friendships and involved in service of others, we are less likely to be led astray and more likely to hear God's voice correctly. The more we are able to soak our hearts and minds in the Scriptures, and the more space we leave in our lives for stillness and reflection, the greater will be our capacity to discern that which is of God. The more yielded we are to God, the easier it will be to discover and do his will (Romans 12:1–2).

We must also develop our prayer lives, asking that God will help us to know his mind and to recognise his voice. In humility Solomon prayed to have a discerning heart so he could distinguish right from wrong (1 Kings 3:9). Paul prayed for the Philippian believers that their love would abound more and more in knowledge and depth of insight so they might discern what was best (Philippians 1:9–10). James tells us that if we are lacking in wisdom we should ask God and it will be given us (James 1:5). A prayerful, God-dependent disposition will go a long way to helping us make sound choices.

Discernment is the ability to distinguish right from wrong, that which is true from that which is false. We are responsible to test what we hear to make sure it is authentic: "Test everything. Hold on to the good. Avoid every kind of evil (1 Thessalonians 5:21)." There are four main ways by which we can discern the voice of God.

Firstly, the Scripture test. God has given us the Bible as an objective basis for discernment. He will never contradict what he has said in Scripture, and he will never add to it. Therefore we can ask ourselves, "Is what I am hearing in line with Scripture? Is it consistent with what I already know about God and his ways? Does it match up with the moral standard of God's Word?" If this is not the case, what we are hearing is not from God.

Secondly, the confirmation test. In important matters of guidance it is always wise to submit what we are thinking to other mature believers who know us well and can help us discern if we are hearing correctly. This may be our church leaders, trusted friends or a mentor/spiritual director. Their job is not to hear God for us but to confirm the validity or otherwise of what we ourselves sense God is saying.

Thirdly, the fruit test. We can ask ourselves, "What will be the result of acting on what I am hearing? Will it produce good fruit in my life and that of others? Does it express the love of God? Will it bring glory and honour to his name?" When we can answer questions like these affirmatively then we are on the right track.

Fourthly, the authenticity test. The genuine voice of God is recognisable because it is the voice of love. It is never harsh, abrasive or condemning but always gentle, caring and encouraging. Yes, it will sometimes challenge or rebuke, but always in a way that builds up and gives hope. When God speaks we are strengthened, inspired and liberated. We can ask, "Does this sound like the God of grace?" Furthermore, the Holy Spirit always speaks to glorify God and honour Jesus. Any genuine word from God will turn the attention away from the speaker so that the focus is on the Father and the Son.

This may seem like a rigorous process, but in discerning God's will it is important that what we are hearing can meet each of the four tests. When that is the case we can move forward with an assurance that we have heard correctly, yet still with humility. While we are wise to be cautious about claiming to have heard God speak, yet we must not be over-cautious either, otherwise we will not respond to God with the spontaneity and joyfulness that should characterise our relationship with him.

❧

Reflection

Why is it important to correctly discern the voice of God?
How can you do that?

SPIRITUAL INSIGHT

❧

Pierre de Caussade and the Sacrament of the Present Moment

Jean Pierre de Caussade (1675–1751) was a priest who was responsible for a retreat house in France, and for providing spiritual direction to a group of nuns, The Sisters of the Visitation. They took notes of his talks and these were eventually published as a book. Long before people were talking about mindfulness, de Caussade was encouraging his followers to be more attentive to themselves, to others, and the world around them by living in the present moment.

Three important themes summarise his teaching:

1. Self-abandonment to divine providence.

By this he meant handing one's self over to the will of God and finding in each moment the presence of God and the guiding hand of his providence. This is best seen in the attitude of Mary, the mother of Jesus: "Let it be to me according to your will (Luke 1:38)." God's will is made known to us moment by moment as the day unfolds. Just as a shadow can hide things from clear view, so God's will is not always clearly visible. Like Mary, we have to know God present in faith, and accept the divine will as it comes to us, often in shadow and darkness.

God's will is often hidden under the ordinary events of every day. He comes to us in "humble disguise". This is why we need to practice awareness.

2. The sacrament of the present moment.

God comes to us as really in the present moment of our lives as he does through the sacraments. In each moment of our lives God is present under the signs of what is ordinary or mundane, so we must be spiritually aware and alert to recognise his presence in what can seem like nothing at all. There is nothing that happens to us in which God cannot be found. What we need are eyes to discern God as God comes to us in each moment—truly present, truly living, truly attentive to the needs of each one.

In whatever our life consists, the will of God comes to us moment by moment.

3. Do what you are doing.

We are to live in the present, doing well what we are doing NOW. Our tendency is to live either in the past or in the future. We do not actually live in the moment, but in moments that have passed or moments yet to come. Thus we are seldom truly present to the present! We must discipline ourselves to find God in life's NOW. If reading is the duty of the moment, then read; if praying is the duty of the moment, then pray; if working, then work: and so on. . . .

A saying associated with de Caussade's teaching summarises his teaching like this: God is NOW and God is HERE or God is NOWHERE.[15]

Here is a prayer-poem based on the idea of being present to God's presence. You can use it to help you become centred on God.

Lord you are here.

Here in *this moment*, here in this place.
Not yesterday, with its memories
Not tomorrow, with its promises
But here now
TODAY
This hour, this moment, this second
Present, near, alongside, within
Here now.

Lord you are here.
Here in this moment, in *this place*.
Not where I used to be, with its comforts
Not where I will be, with its challenges,
But here now
IN THIS PLACE
In this room, at this chair, before this page
Present, near, alongside, within
Here now.

Yes, child, I am here.
Here in this moment, here in this place.
Always present, ever near
Closer than you think;
Holding you
Sustaining you
Giving you life
Listening, speaking, imparting.
This is my Name:
I AM.

Father, I hear you.
Here in this moment, here in this place.
You are here, the eternal I AM
Your word my light
Your presence my strength
I rest contented
At peace
At home
In you. 🌿

Part 5

CLEOPAS, AND THE MOMENT OF RECOGNITION

¹³ Now that same day two of them were going to a village called Emmaus, about seven miles from Jerusalem. ¹⁴ They were talking with each other about everything that had happened. ¹⁵ As they talked and discussed these things with each other, Jesus himself came up and walked along with them; ¹⁶ but they were kept from recognizing him.

¹⁷ He asked them, "What are you discussing together as you walk along?"

They stood still, their faces downcast. ¹⁸ One of them, named Cleopas, asked him, "Are you the only one visiting Jerusalem who does not know the things that have happened there in these days?"

¹⁹ "What things?" he asked.

"About Jesus of Nazareth," they replied. "He was a prophet, powerful in word and deed before God and all the people. ²⁰ The chief priests and our rulers handed him over to be sentenced to death, and they crucified him; ²¹ but we had hoped that he was the one who was going to redeem Israel. And what is more, it is the third day since all this took place. ²² In addition, some of our women amazed us. They went to the tomb early this morning ²³ but didn't find his body. They came and told us that they had seen a vision of angels, who said he was alive. ²⁴ Then some of our companions went to the tomb and found it just as the women had said, but they did not see Jesus."

²⁵ He said to them, "How foolish you are, and how slow to believe all that the prophets have spoken! ²⁶ Did not the Messiah have to suffer these things and then enter his glory?" ²⁷ And beginning with Moses and all the Prophets, he explained to them what was said in all the Scriptures concerning himself.

²⁸ As they approached the village to which they were going, Jesus continued on as if he were going farther. ²⁹ But they urged him strongly, "Stay with us, for it is nearly evening; the day is almost over." So he went in to stay with them.

³⁰ When he was at the table with them, he took bread, gave thanks, broke it and began to give it to them. ³¹ Then their eyes were opened and they recognized him, and he disappeared from their sight. ³² They asked each other, "Were not our hearts burning within us while he talked with us on the road and opened the Scriptures to us?"

³³ They got up and returned at once to Jerusalem. There they found the Eleven and those with them, assembled together ³⁴ and saying, "It is true! The Lord has risen and has appeared to Simon." ³⁵ Then the two told what had happened on the way, and how Jesus was recognized by them when he broke the bread.

|21|

CLEOPAS' STORY

The beautifully crafted narrative of the Emmaus road journey is one of the best loved stories in the whole Bible because it speaks to us on so many different levels, but little is known about the central character, Cleopas, or his mysterious companion. It is a story full of raw emotion with which we can easily identify; a story that has a sad beginning but a very happy ending.

All we can say for sure about Cleopas is that he was a devoted follower of Jesus who was well known to the disciples of Jesus and very much part of their inner circle. In Luke's account of the events around the crucifixion we read about the Eleven (the twelve original disciples minus Judas) and "all the others" who were with them (Luke 24:9 and 33). That Cleopas was welcomed into this close-knit and (at the time) self-protective community suggests that he was regarded highly by the apostles, and that he shared their level of commitment to Jesus as teacher and Lord. It is possible he had been part of the 72 sent out in pairs by Jesus (Luke 10:1), and had probably been in Jerusalem for the events of the previous week. That we now see him turning around and heading for home suggests he was on the verge of giving up, a major crisis in his faith.

But who was his companion on the road? Since no name is given it could have been either male or female. If it was a man it might have been his brother, or close friend, possibly even the person he was paired up with when they were sent out two-by-two on mission by Jesus. The relationship between them seems to have been very close, full of trust and vulnerability. If his companion was female then it would certainly have been his wife, a possibility strengthened by their invitation "Stay with us" (Luke 24:29) which might indicate a shared home. Either way we cannot be certain.

Some scholars believe that Cleopas is the Clopas mentioned in John 19:25: "Near the cross of Jesus stood his mother, his mother's sister, Mary the wife of Clopas, and Mary Magdalene." If this is true then his wife (Mary) had experienced the trauma of the crucifixion first-hand, which explains the depth of their shock and sorrow at what had happened. Early church tradition takes things a little further, suggesting that Cleopas was actually the brother of Joseph, and therefore uncle to Jesus. Such a close family connection would of course have heightened the sense of tragedy that the couple felt as they trudged their way back to Emmaus that afternoon.

For the purpose of this study I will simply refer to Cleopas and his friends as "the two disciples" and let you come to your own conclusions about who they might have been. What we do know is that they had invested themselves heavily in following Jesus (emotionally, spiritually and possibly financially) but had now given up hope and are returning to their familiar surroundings. They are the first of the followers of Jesus to quit and leave the city of Jerusalem. Their rabbi is dead and their hopes have been buried with him. As they walk they are deep in discussion about all that had happened when they are joined by a stranger: "Jesus himself came up and walked along with them, but they were kept from recognising him (v. 15)."

It is at this point that this story intersects with our theme. As we have been pondering how we can grow in our awareness of the presence of God we naturally find ourselves wondering why it was that these two experienced disciples, who must have known Jesus very well indeed, failed to recognise Jesus. Does their lack of recognition have anything to say to us about our own inability to discern the presence of Jesus? And can we learn from their mistake? In the next chapter we will suggest some possible reasons for their failure to recognise Jesus and consider how we might find ourselves in a similar position.

Fortunately we know that this story has a wonderfully positive outcome. Eventually their minds are opened and they realise that the stranger is in fact Jesus. To the importance of *seeing,* and *hearing,* we can now add another strand in spiritual awareness—that of *understanding.* In particular we will identify three major factors that brought them understanding and helped them overcome their temporary blindness. Each of these we can build into our own lives to make us more spiritually receptive. The three factors (the power of friendship, the opened Scriptures and the breaking of bread) will be the subject of later chapters.

Cleopas is not a major figure in the New Testament but his story is recorded here at length because he was an eyewitness of the resurrection. As such he would have told his story many times and become a well-known figure in the fledgeling church. For us, the truth that he at first did not recognise the risen Jesus may help us to feel less badly about our similar failures; the truth that he got there in the end gives us hope that we also can become more adept as spotting the presence of Jesus in our daily lives.

Reflection

Have you ever found yourself in a time of doubt or disappointment? What were the reasons, and how did you respond?

|22|

POOR RECOGNITION

※

I met some people recently whom I know reasonably well, but meeting them out of context, and not expecting to see them, I failed to recognise them. It was embarrassing! Perhaps there is something about this in the failure of Cleopas and his companion to recognise Jesus. They were not expecting to see him, for they believed him to be dead. Maybe, too, his post-resurrection appearance had changed him slightly. Certainly, they were not alone in failing to register the presence of the risen Lord (John 20:14 and 21:4).

However, there seems to have been something more here. Luke chose his words carefully and said "they were kept from recognising him (v. 16)." There was a restraint upon them, a force holding them back and preventing them from recognising Jesus. Although a few commentators say they were kept from recognising him by God, it seems most likely that the hindrance was to be found within themselves. Their state of heart and mind as they trudged wearily home was what held them back. Certainly, they were downcast (v. 17). Their body language spoke of defeat and despair. They were sad-faced, dejected, and morose. They were looking downwards, rather than around, and too consumed by their own concerns to look properly at the stranger who had drawn alongside them.

When we think about what they had gone through we can sympathise with their self-preoccupation. Most of us, when we are troubled, turn inwards upon ourselves and withdraw from others. Ruth Hayley Barton describes their situation well. She writes,

> "These disciples had lost so much more than just a friend. Their dream of what the kingdom of God would look like as they had imagined it … the hopes and dreams around which they had oriented the last three years of their life … the vision that had caused them to give up fishing and tax collecting and the like in order to commit themselves to following Jesus … it was all gone."[16]

No wonder they were absorbed in their own thoughts.

As much as we may sympathise with the two disciples, the truth is that self-absorption like this can easily rob us of our spiritual perception. What happens at such times is that our spirit (the part of us that can recognise and respond to God) is subsumed within our soul (the seat of our mind, emotions and will) and can no longer function freely. We become weighed down inside and our spirit is no longer free to respond to the Holy Spirit. We are held back by the heaviness within us. When we look carefully at the story, we can see three ways in which this had happened to these two disciples.

Firstly, they are wrapped up in their own thoughts, ideas and assumptions about what has happened—the *mind* can mislead us. Their understanding of Jesus up till this point, like many of his followers, was that he would be a political Messiah who would overthrow the Romans. When this did not happen and he was instead crucified they lost all hope, and as we know, "hope deferred makes the heart sick (Proverbs 13:12)." They could not conceive of a suffering Messiah. The death of Jesus could only spell defeat. Their words reveal their shattered expectations and betray their illusions: "We had hoped that he was going to redeem Israel (v. 21)." So much of our pain is caused by wrong thinking, and so many of our difficulties with God are due to us making wrong assumptions about what he will do and how he will act.

relatable

Furthermore, their minds were closed to certain possibilities. Despite all that Jesus had said about rising again, they could only conceive that his death would mean the end of their dream. So when the women returned excitedly from the empty tomb, they were "amazed" (v. 22)—in the sense of being astonished—that anyone could think Jesus might have risen. In their cynical mind-set, if the women had not actually seen him alive then he could not be risen (v. 24). Again, if we are rigid in our thinking, locked into our preconceived ideas and closed to anything outside our established parameters, we will find it harder to see what God is doing. He often seems to work outside the boundaries of human thinking!

do we really expect to see god beside us?

Secondly, they are absorbed by sadness, grief, loss, disappointment and confusion—our *emotions* can overwhelm us. They had been traumatised by what had happened to Jesus. Seeing the crucifixion had wounded them deeply, they were scarred emotionally. Their feelings understandably overwhelm them. We cannot minimise the impact of any kind of bereavement or loss, especially when it has been traumatic. It is not healthy to deny our emotions or to bottle them up. They need to be acknowledged and expressed appropriately. It takes time to recover from major painful events and sometimes that means that we may feel spiritually numb, out of touch with God and unable to sense his presence as we normally would. We must be patient with ourselves because the process cannot be rushed, but we must not allow pain to overwhelm us. We must give space for God to heal us, and in due time give us grace to let go and move on.

Thirdly, they are trapped in unbelief, unwilling to believe the clear testimony of Scripture—our *will* can hold us back. Jesus listened carefully to all that they had to say but his verdict was clear: "How foolish you are and how slow of heart to believe all that the prophets have spoken! Did not the Christ have to suffer these things and then enter his glory (vv. 25–26)?" This slowness of heart is more than an inability to understand, it is a stubborn refusal to accept the truth because the truth is sometimes unpalatable and often inconvenient. Jon Bloom writes, "Their outward inability to recognize Jesus mirrored their inward unbelief of what the Scriptures revealed about him."[17]

They did not want to allow for the possibility of a suffering Messiah and they were not attracted to a discipleship that might also involve suffering for them. Our own dislike of pain and desire to remove all elements of risk from life can blind us to the true nature of discipleship, so clearly taught in the Bible and epitomised in the call of Jesus to take up our cross and follow him (Mark 8:34–35). In this the church often colludes with the world by offering a gospel free of suffering. When those brought up on a spiritual diet that promises only blessings encounter suffering first-hand, they are often thrown into total confusion. They wonder "Has God has left me?", or "Is he punishing me?" instead of asking, "Where is God in this situation? How can this draw me closer to him?" They are blinded to the presence of the One who draws alongside us in our time of need, imagining rather that he has left them.

Mercifully, the two disciples were not alone in their struggle. The God of all comfort and the Father of mercies was aware of their need. The One who promised beauty for ashes, the oil of joy for mourning and a garment of praise for heaviness took note of them (Isaiah 61:3). That's why, at their moment of need, along came a stranger to help them.

*

Reflection

Why can self-absorption easily rob us of our spiritual perception? Has this ever been an issue for you? What is the answer?

|23|

THE POWER OF FRIENDSHIP

Counsellors love this story in Luke 24, particularly the place where it says, "Jesus himself came up and walked with them (v. 15)." Why? Because here Jesus demonstrates the best practice when it comes to listening to others. What else would we expect from the Wonderful Counsellor? His example is a good one to follow. The verse actually says this: "drawing near he journeyed with them." In their moment of brokenness and heartache they find they were not alone. The Saviour had drawn alongside them to become their companion on the journey.

I love the way in which Jesus simply fell into step with them, joining them where they were on the road and adopting their chosen pace. There was no big fanfare, nor any dramatic announcement. In fact, so gentle was his arrival, they barely noticed his presence. What an example of humility, self-effacement and servanthood for any people helper! What a gift to be able to focus on others and not draw attention to oneself!

After walking with them for a while without saying a word, Jesus spoke, although they did not recognise him. His questions are simple, open-ended and designed to draw them out. "What are you discussing?" he asks, and then again for extra clarification, "What things?" He was not being nosey. He wanted to hear their story, because our stories matter, and it is important that we can give voice to them. Slowly, their painful account of recent events emerged and, as he listened attentively, he gained their confidence. Soon, he would be able to share with them truths that will help them recover.

This story is also an incredible illustration of the power of friendship and the importance of relationships in helping us grow closer to God. Friendship is a basic human need without which we remain lonely and isolated. Writer Tom Rath says that, ". . . friendships are among the most fundamental of human needs. The fact is, we are biologically predisposed to this need for relationships, and our environment accentuates this every day. Without friends it is very difficult for us to get by, let alone thrive."[18] The Bible also celebrates the connection between friendship and well-being when it says, "Two are better than one, because they have a good return for their labour: if either of them falls down, one can help the other up. But pity anyone who falls and has no-one to help them up (Ecclesiastes 4:9–10)."

The two disciples seem to share such a life-giving friendship. We could describe them as "soul friends", people who connect deeply with each other in a way that includes a spiritual dimension. It is heartening to see that they are deep in conversation as they walk together, sharing their innermost thoughts and feelings about all that has happened with each other. This is one of the best ways to process hurt and pain.

It appears to have been a sparky conversation. Three different words are used to describe their dialogue, each of which adds another description of what was happening. First, they are said to be *talking* with one another (v. 14), then they are *discussing* (v. 15, suggesting a lot of interaction asking questions and sharing ideas), then they are *exchanging* with each other (v. 17, a word suggesting a throwing backwards and forwards with force). We can imagine a healthy, robust conversation that clears the air, provides some catharsis and yet brings them closer together. The best of friendships allow for such honest conversations and it is an exchange in which Jesus is happy to be involved.

What is striking about their friendship, however, is that even in their pain it is not exclusive or restrictive. Almost without realizing what they are doing they welcome a stranger into the discussion, and reveal to him some of their deepest concerns. So many friendships are cliquish and protective, designed to shut others out, but not this one; there is room for another, and it is that welcome that will transform their situation, for the stranger is Jesus. Their openness is all the more beautiful to see because they consider him to be just another visitor to Jerusalem from whom they will gain nothing; yet their acceptance of him will prove to be a great blessing to them. No wonder the Bible speaks about the benefits of welcoming strangers (Hebrews 13:2, Matthew 25:35). We often find ourselves learning more about God through the most unlikely of people, and when we least expect it.

Not only are the two welcoming of the stranger but they are also hospitable. As the day draws to a close, they invite him to stay with them. This is not simply a polite invitation in accordance with Jewish custom but a genuine offer springing from a desire to spend time with their new friend: "they urged him strongly (v. 29)." Because their hearts are opened, so too is their home. Notice there is no presumption on the part of Jesus here: "He acted as if he were going further (v. 28)"—a reminder to us that the Saviour never forces his presence upon us but waits to be invited. Hospitality is an important aspect of what we may call spiritual friendship. It may occasionally involve the offer of a bed for the night and a place to stay, but more often than not it is the provision of a simple meal and a warm welcome, or the sharing of a coffee around the kitchen table with an opportunity to talk. Always though it requires the hospitality of the heart—a listening ear, an accepting presence and the occasional hug.

It was the British monastic Aelred of Rievaulx (1110–1167) who gave us what I consider to be the best definition of spiritual friendship when he wrote: "You and I are here, and I hope that Christ is between us as a third."[19] Writer Keith Anderson gives this a contemporary feel when he speaks about "a particular kind of companionship in which two or more people walk together in heightened awareness of the presence of yet another, the Holy Spirit, who is the living presence of God."[20] This is certainly what we are seeing played out in this story between the two friends and Jesus, and it is something to be cultivated in our own relationships.

Not all friendships will be able to reach this this level of intimacy of course, but a few can, and if we are to deepen our walk with God then we must cultivate such friendships. No friendship simply happens. We choose our friends, and then we invest time in those relationships. If you have such friends, thank God for them, and let your friends know you appreciate them. If as yet you don't have this kind of friendship, ask God to provide it for you and be on the lookout for the kind of people who might meet this need in your life.

I am grateful to God for the friends God has given me over the years, whose friendship and love have helped me to hear his voice, be more aware of his presence in my life and understand more clearly what he is doing in my life. Only yesterday I spent quality time with some of my closest spiritual "buddies", friends with whom I have been connected for more than a decade. We were able to talk openly, be honest and vulnerable with each other, and the conversation was cathartic and healing, as well as amusing. It was an important day for me as once again I encountered Christ in the midst of human friendship and found myself refreshed and revitalized for my ongoing spiritual journey. We shared our stories, felt we had been heard and understood, and then went on our way rejoicing.

Reflection

Do you have good friends? How can you develop spiritual friendships?
Are you a good friend to others?

|24|

THE OPENED SCRIPTURES

Only when Jesus has really listened to the story of the two disciples does he enter into the conversation, and he does so in order to bolster their faith and change their thinking. While it is essential to sympathise with those who are hurting, sometimes at the right moment, and always with tenderness and love, it is appropriate to challenge any wrong ideas that may be hindering recovery and replace them with the truth that brings healing. This is what lies behind the intervention of Jesus.

Jesus does not mince his words. He challenges them on two counts—their lack of understanding and their failure to believe what should have been clear and plain from their knowledge of the Old Testament prophets (v. 25). Their interpretation of the weekend's events was wrong because they were looking at them through the lens of their pre-conceived idea that the Messiah would be a political figure who would overthrow the Romans. How could they believe the report of the women that Jesus was risen when it was outside the scope of their understanding and beyond their very limited faith? They were indeed "foolish" and "slow of heart to believe". The rebuke serves as a wake-up call to them.

Jesus begins by explaining to them what the Scriptures actually have to say about the Messiah. "Did not the Christ have to suffer these things and then enter into his glory?" he asks. Suffering is fundamental to the mission and calling of the Messiah, so they should not be surprised by what had happened. Far from contradicting the idea that Jesus was the promised Messiah, the fact of his suffering confirms his identity, if they will only think about it. Then he shows them how this was clearly taught in all the Scriptures. He begins with Moses and the books of the law, and then moves on to what had been written by the prophets. It must have been a wonderfully comprehensive survey of the Old Testament, and a master-class in scriptural interpretation. Yet, even though he is showing them "the things concerning himself" the two disciples at this point still remain blind to the fact that the stranger, in talking about the Christ, is actually talking about himself; and they have still to recognise that their travelling companion is none other than the risen Jesus.

We cannot be sure exactly which Scriptures Jesus expounded to them, and it is beyond the scope of this book to examine in detail all the possibilities. Since he was concerned to show them that the Messiah would of necessity suffer, he may have pointed them to Psalm 22 for example, which begins with words that Jesus had uttered from the cross "My God, my God, why have you forsaken me?" (v. 1) and which contains a vivid description of the events of the crucifixion and its attendant agonies. He may also have reminded them of the description of the Suffering Servant in Isaiah 53:1–12, a person "despised and rejected by men, a man of sorrows and acquainted with suffering (v. 3)." Again, this passage predicts the events of the cross with startling accuracy. It speaks about him being pierced (v. 5), being silent as lamb (v. 7), suffering innocently (v. 9), being numbered with the transgressors (v. 12), praying for his persecutors (v. 12) and finally being assigned a grave with the rich (v. 9). More than that, it also interprets his violent death as something willed by God (v. 10), a vicarious offering that would bring peace and healing to others (vv. 5

and 10) and through which many would be justified (v. 11).

The more the stranger speaks, the more attentive the two disciples become, and the greater the impact of his words upon them. Something is stirred within them, a feeling they have not experienced before, but which they cannot deny. Later they will recall what happened with these words: "Were not our hearts burning within us while he talked to us on the road and opened the Scriptures to us (v. 32)?" This burning sensation was nothing to do with indigestion! It was a sign that the words of God were impacting their souls in a deep way. As they listened to the Scriptures being opened to their understanding something was kindled within them—a renewed love for God and an awareness of his presence. The fire of love that had almost gone out was sparked into life again by the word of God being explained to them simply and clearly.

The Scriptures have the power to awaken us to the reality of God. When applied to our lives by the Holy Spirit they become living and active, sharper than the sharpest sword, piercing through our defences and reaching the deepest part of us with liberating truth (Hebrews 4:12). They have the ability to teach us the truth, expose our wrong thinking, then point us in the right way so that we are trained and equipped to do God's will (2 Timothy 4:16–17). For this reason they are foundational to Christian living and spiritual formation, and we neglect them at our peril. The dangerous trend of elevating experience above Scripture has to be resisted, as does the tendency to think we can manage with only a shallow interaction with God's word. Sidelining the Bible in favour of worship experience is an extremely unhelpful trendency in the contemporary church. Our lives must be built upon the objectivity of Scripture and to be spiritually healthy and robust we must lay up God's word in our hearts like the treasure it is (Psalm 119:11, Colossians 3:16).

The two disciples had only the Old Testament record to turn to, and even then they did not possess it in the way that we can own the Scriptures today, in our own language and in contemporary style. We have the full revelation of God available to us. The Old Testament points to Jesus, the Gospels describe Jesus and the epistles explain Jesus. We can hold the book in our hands. We can turn to it whenever we want. We have the opportunity to read it, study it, meditate upon it, and respond to it. We become attentive to God as we thoughtfully interact with the text, and as we do so we are changed and transformed. Eugene Peterson puts it well when he writes, "Christians feed on Scripture. Holy Scripture nurtures the holy community as food nurtures the human body. Christians don't simply learn or study or use Scripture; we assimilate it, take it into our lives in such a way that it gets metabolized into acts of love, cups of cold water, missions into all the world, healing and evangelism and justice in Jesus' name, hands raised in adoration of the Father, feet washed in company with the Son."[21]

Some of us have the high privilege of teaching the Scriptures to others. We must pray for that anointing of God that will enable us to "open" the Scriptures in such a way that their life-changing power is communicated to others. We are to do the thorough work of preparation through our study and research and then pray that God will open our own eyes so that we can find Jesus within the sacred page and so help others to do the same. It is not about drawing attention to ourselves, showing how clever we are or sharing our homespun wisdom but of pointing to Jesus. We must take seriously the injunction that Paul gave to the young leader, Timothy: "Do your best to present yourself to God as one approved, a workman who does not need to be ashamed and who correctly handles the word of truth (2 Timothy 2:15)." There can be no excuse for laziness or sloppy work when we have such a ministry to fulfil, or of getting in the way of the Spirit's work of revealing Jesus.

All of us must make sure we give attention to the Scriptures whether in public gatherings or in private devotion for in attending to them we attend to the voice of God and meet the person of Christ. Is this what Paul meant when he further encouraged Timothy to devote himself to the public reading of Scripture (1 Timothy 4:13)? We must listen to Scripture as if we are hearing the very words of God and encounter it with the same aspiration as if we were meeting Christ himself. I have been reading Scripture now for over fifty years, so I guess I know the Bible fairly well, but I have this confession to make: I wish I had read it even more, and in greater depth than I have. There are things I do not understand about the Bible, and often I am perplexed by what it appears to say. I concede that it is not an easy book to read. But it has spoken to me so many times over the years, and met me at my point of need on so many occasions that I have no doubt whatsoever concerning its divine origins. I am continually amazed at its relevance to my own life in the 21st Century and taken aback by the ability of its stories to speak to people with contemporary wisdom and insight so many hundreds of years later.

Richard Foster has shared how, along with others working on the project, after five years of intensive work in producing the RENOVARE Spiritual Formation Bible, they came to the conclusion that the unity of the Bible is seen in the development of a life with God which is centred on the person of Jesus. He writes, "Through Scripture we heard God whispering down through the centuries: 'I am *with* you!' 'I am *with* you!' 'I am *with* you!' Then, we heard God asking a question that searches the human person to the depths: 'Are you willing to be with Me?' The Scripture reveals that saying 'yes' to this invitation thrusts human beings into life with God . . . daily . . . hourly . . . moment by moment." (his italics)[22]

The two disciples on the Emmaus road heard that same whisper as Jesus revealed the Scriptures to them, and slowly, gradually, it lifted them out of their despair and set them on their way again. We too can hear the still, small voice of God whenever we choose to become attentive to Scripture. We can pray the words of a hymn from long ago: "Beyond the sacred page, I seek Thee Lord; My spirit longs for Thee, Thou Living Word."[23] It is a prayer the Holy Spirit, our divine Teacher, loves to answer.

Reflection

What part does the Bible play in your life?
Do you spend enough time in the Scriptures?

|25|

THE BREAKING OF BREAD

The time on the journey homewards to Emmaus must have passed quickly as the two friends enjoyed such deep and stimulating conversation with their new companion. His unfolding of the Scriptures had touched them deeply and they were now in a much better frame of mind. Their spirits had lifted, and they felt a glimmer of hope in their hearts, although they had still not realised it was Jesus walking with them.

As they approach the village the stranger gives every appearance of continuing on his own journey, but the two friends, aware of the late hour, implore him to stay with them. This is not simply out of politeness or Middle Eastern courtesy. They genuinely want to welcome him into their home and spend more time with him. The discussion has whetted their appetite for more. Given this blend of sincere friendship and warm hospitality the stranger gladly joins them.

We may wonder why Jesus made such a deliberate show of going on his way, for that is the sense conveyed by the words "Jesus *acted* as if he were going further (v. 28, my italics)." We cannot know for certain but it seems there is no presumption on his part that he will stay the night with them. He does not take their friendship or hospitality for granted, but waits to be invited. He had brought them so far on their journey of understanding, but now waits to see if they want to know more. This seems to be characteristic of how Jesus relates to us. He never forces his presence upon us, never pushes us further than we want to go, and never transgresses our freewill. He gives us the freedom to choose to open our hearts to him, without coercion, but when we do he is more than ready to join us right where we are.

Once they have settled in they make preparations for a meal together and it is here that things become really interesting. The stranger apparently breaks all the rules of etiquette by offering the prayer of thanksgiving for the bread: "he took the bread, gave thanks, broke it and began to give it to them (v. 30)." This would normally be the responsibility of the head of the house. The stranger who had become their companion and teacher and then their friend now becomes their host. This unusual behaviour would certainly have aroused their attention. Even as he is speaking something remarkable happens—"their eyes were opened and they recognised him (v. 31)." All hindrance to their seeing is removed and the blinkers are lifted. Suddenly it all makes sense. No wonder their hearts had been on fire when he was explaining the Scriptures about a suffering Messiah to them. He had been speaking about himself. Their guest is none other than Jesus, crucified yes, but now risen. Later they would testify to this very fact, that it was in the breaking of bread that Jesus was made known to them (v. 35). Something about the way he spoke, the way he acted, had triggered a familiar memory that caused their eyes to be opened.

The expression "breaking bread" on one level means nothing more than a simple meal shared together with others. In Jewish custom the taking of food was accompanied by a formal pronouncing of blessing over the bread that was to be eaten, followed by breaking the loaf in two and then sharing it with those at the table. In some ways this practice is akin to saying grace before a meal but with more solemnity and greater significance. Many times the disciples would have seen Jesus take this role, sometimes when they were on their own, often when they were guests in the house of others, such as at the home of Mary, Martha and Lazarus in Bethany. Perhaps Jesus had a unique way of blessing the bread, and the two friends recognised this as he lifted up the loaf and prayed. Maybe as his hands were raised they saw the nail marks. Whatever happened, through the ordinary practice of sharing a meal together, they became aware of his true identity.

We have mentioned already that sharing a meal together can be central in cultivating the kind of friendship that helps us become more aware of God. In the relaxed setting of a meal, in welcoming and enjoyable company, conversation can flow freely and hearts can be opened to one another and to God. True fellowship can take place. When Luke says Jesus "was at table with them (v. 30)" he is not thinking of guests sitting rather formally around a dining table, but of the Jewish custom (adopted from the Romans) of reclining at table on couches designed for comfort and relaxation. This is the setting in which the two friends finally recognise Jesus. Spending time together over a meal becomes the setting for spiritual revelation. This kind of intimate fellowship in the company of others who desire to know God more deeply is something we must build into our own lives because it will help us become more spiritually aware.

There is a real sense in which any meal eaten with thankfulness to God is a sacred meal, but Luke hints at a deeper dimension to what was happening in the Emmaus home that evening. His careful use of words suggests that he wants his readers to be reminded of the Last Supper and the way Jesus shared the Passover meal with his disciples. When he says that Jesus "took bread, gave thanks, broke it and began to give it to them (v. 30)" he is repeating almost word for word what Jesus did in the Upper Room: "And he took bread, gave thanks, and broke it, and gave it to them, saying, 'This is my body given for you; do this in remembrance of me (Luke 22:19).'" The same four actions are described and in the same order, which is clearly no accident.

Luke is wanting to tell his readers that in observing the Lord's Supper we too can also have our eyes opened to the presence of Jesus.

It is interesting that Jesus chose to be remembered by his followers in the sharing of a meal together. In the New Testament "the breaking of bread" refers both to an ordinary meal as well as what is commonly called communion or the Eucharist. Indeed it seems that it was in the context of a love feast or fellowship meal that the first believers usually celebrated the Lord's Supper, an ordinary meal leading seamlessly into a most sacred one. Thus we read in the Acts that they devoted themselves to "the apostles' teaching and to the fellowship, to the breaking of bread and to prayer (2:42)", and also that they "broke bread in their homes and ate together with glad and sincere hearts (2:46)." Clearly both the formal remembering of Christ's death through a special meal, and the more informal sharing of fellowship over food, are both intended to be means of grace to us. Both can be occasions when the presence of Christ is made known to us.

American priest and writer Tish Harrison Warren, in seeking to discover God in the ordinariness of life, has written of how in the most simple of daily left-over meals we can become conscious that Christ is our bread and gives us bread. Every meal we eat points us to him who is our true food and source of eternal nourishment. She says, "The Eucharist—our gathered meal of thanksgiving for the life, death, and resurrection of Christ—transforms each humble meal into a moment to recall that we receive all of life, from soup to salvation, by grace. As such, these small, daily moments are sacramental—not that they are sacraments themselves, but that God meets us in and through the earthy, material world in which we dwell."[24] When we awaken to this possibility, we awaken ourselves to the presence of God in the daily routines of ordinary life.

We must also consider here the way in which sharing in the communion service can increase our awareness of God. Jesus said, "Do this in remembrance of me (Luke 22:19, 1 Corinthinas 11:24–

25)." Through the broken bread and the shared cup we are visibly and sensibly reminded of the central facts of our faith that Christ's body was broken for us and his blood shed on our behalf. By participating in this sacred ritual we can be made conscious once again of all that Christ has achieved for us through his death at Calvary. That frequent reminder of something so important must provide a significant help for us as regards our spiritual wakefulness. No wonder taking part was a basic spiritual practice within the early church (Acts 2:42).

There is more to it than this, however. Something is actually communicated to us when we eat the bread and drink the cup. Evangelical Protestants in particular are wary of any idea of transubstantiation (whereby the elements are said to be transformed into the actual body and blood of Christ), preferring to think of communion simply as a sacrament, which is simply an outward and visible sign of an inward and spiritual grace. This can mean that our approach to receiving communion can be somewhat shallow and lacking in expectation, and yet the apostle Paul would lift our sights much higher. He says, "Is not the cup of thanksgiving for which we give thanks a participation in the blood of Christ? And is not the bread that we break a participation in the body of Christ (1 Corinthians 10:16–17)?" To both questions he expects a resounding "Yes!" The implication is clear: there is spiritual blessing to be received when we eat and drink by faith, being mindful of what we are doing. It is far more than just a memorial meal.

I would go so far as to say something of Christ's risen presence can be made known to us, especially when we approach communion with an understanding of what we are doing and an expectation of receiving spiritual blessing. We do not have to believe in transubstantiation to believe that Christ is really present, and that in receiving communion something of his life is communicated to us. The somewhat mysterious words of Jesus in John 6:53–54 seem to bear this out: "I tell you the truth, unless you can eat the flesh of the Son of Man and drink his blood, you have no life in you. Whoever eats my flesh and drinks my blood has eternal life, and I will raise him up at the last day." The challenge for us is to become increasingly present to his Presence whenever we meet together in his name (Matthew 18:20), and in particular when we meet to share fellowship through communion.

Returning to the story in Luke 24 we may be somewhat disappointed to discover that as soon as the two disciples recognised Jesus "he disappeared from their sight (v. 31)." It seems like an anti-climax after such a struggle to become aware of his identity, yet it seems they did not feel this way. Their faith has been dramatically revived and these formerly dispirited disciples have been revitalised. Immediately they return to Jerusalem, despite the late hour and the dangers of travelling by night. They cannot wait to get back to their friends and add their witness to that of others: Jesus really is alive again! There is no need for Jesus to remain physically with them now for their hearts have caught fire again and soon the Spirit will be poured out upon them on the day of Pentecost. They will be able to tell their story again and again to encourage others also to believe.

A story that began with such a sense of loss and dejection has been transformed by the presence of Jesus into one of joy and certainty. We have seen for ourselves how we also can become more aware of that same presence through the power of friendship, the opened Scriptures and the breaking of bread. God wants us to know him deeply and be aware of his nearness, and if we desire that blessing for ourselves he will make sure we are not disappointed.

⚘

Reflection
What thoughts do you have about communion (the Lord's Supper)?
What place does it hold in your life?

SPIRITUAL INSIGHT

❦

Brother Lawrence and Practicing the Presence of God

Brother Lawrence (whose birth name was Nicholas Herman) was born into a poor family in France in 1611. He served as a soldier, and also a footman, before entering a Carmelite monastery in Paris in 1666, where he served as a Lay brother and worked in the kitchens. He is remembered for the book *The Practice of the Presence of God*, published after his death by a friend and considered a classic within the history of spirituality. It contains notes from their conversations as well as letters written by Brother Lawrence and explores the theme of how he came to enjoy the presence of God in a remarkable way.

Brother Lawrence first encountered God in a way similar to Jeremiah, through something he saw. When he was 18, he came across a dry and lifeless tree in the depths of winter, and as he considered this God spoke to him, reminding him that in a short time, with the coming of spring, the tree would be renewed and once again bear leaves, flowers and fruit. Perhaps something stirred deep within him about the change God wanted to bring into his own life. From that point on he had a deep awareness of God and determined that he would live his life as a response to God's love. In particular, he desired to be continually aware of God's presence.

During his time in the monastery he worked in the kitchens, but in this noisy and busy environment he began to learn how to live in God's presence by fixing his mind as much as possible on God and by enjoying a constant conversation with him. Long before there was any teaching about mindfulness Brother Lawrence recognised the importance of disciplining the mind and choosing what to think about. Like everyone he struggled with wandering thoughts but trained himself, whenever his mind would wander, to bring it back to where he wanted it to be—the contemplation of God. This took many years, and he was very honest about his struggles, but by persevering he eventually came to the place where it was easier for him to think about God than not to do so. There amongst the rattle of the pots and pans and the steam of the kitchen he cultivated his relationship with God.

For Brother Lawrence there was no distinction between his work in the kitchens and his life of prayer since everything he did, he did for the love of God. His work was his prayer, and done in dependency on God. He knew very well that he could not live a life of communion with God without his help. Famously he said, "The time of business does not with me differ from the time of prayer; and in the noise and clatter of my kitchen, while several persons are at the same time calling for different things, I possess God in as great tranquillity as if I were upon my knees at the blessed sacrament."[25]

Brother Lawrence developed a way of talking with God throughout his day, what he described as an habitual, silent and secret conversation of the soul with God. Of course he had to focus on his work, and concentrate on the task in hand, but in intervals of quiet he would allow his heart to turn towards God again. These little moments of adoration kept his soul in tune with God. He reasoned that if we would not leave a friend alone who came to visit us, why would we want to neglect God who was always near us? Repeated, small acts of inward worship throughout the day are sufficient to cultivate in us an awareness of God.

The impact of this closeness to God on his life was visible to those who knew him well. He seemed to possess a calmness of soul even in the busiest of times, and a quiet joy that drew others to him. Many came to seek his advice and to learn the secret of his inner life. He recommended no method or magical formula however, only an unreserved surrender to God and an unremitting desire to love God above all else.

Surely there is something here we can learn from Brother Lawrence, even in the hectic days in which we live? Yes, it is easy to be distracted and lose our focus on God; yes, we are prone to inattentiveness and to not noticing the God whose presence is all around us; but if we truly desire to know God more deeply and to become increasingly aware of his nearness, then we shall find it. "God is everywhere," said Brother Lawrence, "in all places, and there is no spot where we cannot draw near to him, and hear him speaking in our heart: with a little love, just a very little, we shall not find it hard."[26]

Conclusion

As we come the end of our journey together in search of a greater awareness of God, we have travelled from the spiritual blindness of Jacob to the sublime communion enjoyed by Brother Lawrence. They represent the two ends of the "attentive to God" spectrum: the one totally unaware of God, the other rapturously engaged with him. Hopefully the stories we have looked at have shown how we ourselves may move along the spectrum to a greater involvement with God. All of us will be somewhere along the spectrum, and where we are will vary from time to time.

What we must bear in mind is that attentiveness to God is not simply the privilege of a chosen few, and it is not beyond the grasp of any who desire a closer walk with God. Neither need our experience of God be confined to Sunday services or midweek gatherings, nor limited to sacred buildings or holy places. God is to be found everywhere and the world around us is bursting with his presence if we have eyes to see, ears to hear, and minds to understand his ways. He is present in our homes and work places, in shopping malls and parks, on lonely beaches and crowded sidewalks, in bustling cities and isolated hamlets, on mountain tops and in traffic jams, in quiet pubs and noisy restaurants, in high rise blocks and in make-shift shelters.... In the ordinariness of our ordinary lives we too can find God and every child of his can live in a growing intimacy with the heavenly Father.

We will need to deal with the root causes of our inattentiveness, and be willing to step aside from the demands of daily life occasionally so that we do not miss the presence of God. We will need to grow in spiritual insight and the ability to hear the voice of God, as well as our understanding of God's ways. One quality we will need to develop is that of perseverance, the ability to keep pursuing our goal of greater attentiveness. Sometimes it will seem relatively easy to be aware of God, another time we will feel all over the place and have no spiritual hunger whatsoever. Don't be alarmed if that is your experience sometimes, for that is quite normal. There is a natural ebb and flow to the spiritual life and no-one lives continually on the mountain top. We need a steady persistence to keep practising the disciplines that will help us draw near to God and over time we will discover that our attentiveness has grown and our awareness deepened. Turning to God and recognising his presence will become something we do instinctively the longer we pursue this goal.

One thing is certain. We will not, however, be able to achieve our goal without God's help, and that is why I want to finish with a prayer, for myself and for my readers. Like Jacob, we will need the grace of divine disclosure.

Prayer for Attentiveness

Lord you know my hunger for you
and I know your desire to make yourself known to me.
Grant me therefore gracious Lord,
eyes to see,
ears to hear,
and a mind to understand your ways.
Cause me to become more aware of you
and more fully attentive to your Presence.
Help me to notice your activity in the world around me
and be responsive to the nudges of your Spirit.
Above all, let my ordinary, little life
be full of you,
for your glory
AMEN. 🌿

QUESTIONS FOR GROUP DISCUSSION

🌿 Part 1: Jacob, and the Problem of Inattentiveness

In preparation read beforehand Part 1 of the book (chapters 1–5).

As you begin the session read together from Genesis 28:10–22.

1. What factors in your personal history/family background affect how you relate to God? Which help you, and which hinder you?
2. In what "place" do you find yourself now? How does the truth that "there is no place where he is not" encourage you today? What insights do you gain from Psalm 139:7–12?
3. What do you think it means to awaken to God's presence? Why is it necessary? What are the benefits of living an awakened life?
4. What are some common reasons for inattentiveness to God? What are your personal reasons? What might help you to be more attentive?
5. How does the knowledge that God is a gracious God who longs to reveal himself to us encourage you to seek to know God more deeply?
6. Do you long to live an awakened life? What do you imagine it might look like?

PRAY together about what you have shared. Be honest and real before God.

PRACTICE: during the coming week try and practice Breathing Prayer as described in the book.

🌿 Part 2: Moses, and the Importance of Turning Aside

In preparation read beforehand Part 2 of the book (chapters 6–10).

As you begin the session read together from Exodus 3:1–10.

1. "The providence of God is at work in the life of every believer, and God is preparing us today for what he wants us to do tomorrow."

How can you see in your own life the way God has ordered the events of your life to bring his purposes to pass?

2. Why do you think we have a tendency to despise the ordinary? What part does "ordinary" play in your daily life? What does it mean to develop a "spirituality of ordinariness"?

3. What does the writer mean by describing God as "the great Attention Grabber"? As you look back on the past week have you been aware at all of God seeking your attention? What happened, and how did you respond?

4. Noticing God requires the willingness to step aside, as Moses did, to stop and look. What works against this willingness to slow down and become more reflective in your own life?

5. If we have eyes to see the ordinary can be made special, and we can encounter God in the ordinary tasks of daily life. What do you think is the meaning behind taking off our shoes, as Moses did?

6. Mediate on Psalm 90:12 – "Teach us to number our days aright, that we may gain a heart of wisdom." Share your thoughts with the group.

PRAY together about what you have shared. Let the desire and longing of your heart come to the surface.

PRACTICE the Prayer of Examen, either in the full version or the shorter form, in the coming week. It may help to journal your thoughts.

✿ Part 3: Jeremiah, and the Gift of Seeing

In preparation read beforehand Part 3 of the book (chapters 11–15).

As you begin the session read together from Jeremiah 1:4–14.

1. When did you first come to know God personally? Share briefly one significant moment in your journey of faith.

2. What encouragement can we take from the story of Jeremiah's call as we seek to be more attentive to God?

3. In what ways can creation speak to us? Why do you think it has been called "God's second book'? Share any experience you have had of

encountering God through creation.

4. What do you understand by the expression "the eyes of your heart"? Of the three ways of seeing spiritually (through mental pictures, dreams and visions), which have you experienced personally? How would you like to develop in this area?

5. What are some of the causes of spiritual eye disease? How can we make sure the lens of our inner eye remains clean and clear?

PRAY together from the words of the apostle Paul in Ephesians 1:17–18. Make his words your own.

PRACTICE: during the coming week make time and space to try an Awareness Walk.

🌿 Part 4: Samuel, and the Posture of Listening

In preparation read beforehand Part 4 of the book (chapters 16–20).

As you begin the session read together from 1 Samuel 3:1–10.

1. Share your experience of hearing God speak to you. Is this something that comes easily to you or not?

2. How does the Bible give us confidence to believe that each of us as God's children has the ability to hear God's voice?

3. What do you understand by the term "posture of listening"? What helped Samuel to hear God's voice, and how can we better prepare ourselves to listen to God?

4. How can we enjoy "an on-going conversation with God"? In what different ways does the Holy Spirit make this possible for us?

5. How may we avoid self-deception when it comes to hearing the voice of God? What tests can we apply to help us discern what God is saying correctly?

PRAY together, asking God to sharpen your ability to hear his voice, basing your confidence on Isaiah 30:21.

PRACTICE: during the coming week read about Pierre de Caussade and *The Sacrament of the Present Moment*. Use his insights to help you become more centred, more relaxed, and therefore more able to hear the still, small voice.

✣ Part 5: Cleopas, and the Moment of Recognition

In preparation read beforehand Part 5 of the book (chapters 21–25).

As you begin the session read together from Luke 24:13–35.

1. Have you ever had a time when you felt like giving up?
2. Why is self-absorption such a factor in despair? Why were the two disciples so downcast?
3. In what ways in this story do we see Jesus as the Wonderful Counsellor? Why is spiritual friendship such an important factor in our growing in spiritual awareness and understanding? How can you develop spiritual friendship in your life?
4. Why does Jesus take the time to explain the Scriptures to the two disciples? How do the Scriptures help us in our spiritual growth and connection with God? How do you currently give place to the Scriptures in your own life?
5. What has been your experience of communion (the Lord's Supper) so far in your Christian life? How can taking part in this sacrament enhance our relationship with God and make us more aware of the presence of Christ. How are your ideas about its meaning affirmed or challenged in chapter 25?

PRAY together that God will open your understanding so you can know him more deeply, using Colossians 1:9 and 2:2 as a starting point.

PRACTICE: during the coming week read about Brother Lawrence and *The Practice of the Presence of God*. Use his insights to help you to be more aware of God in your daily life.

✿ NOTES

1 Ben Campbell Johnson, *Living before God: Deepening Our Sense of Divine Presence* (Grand Rapids: Eerdmans, 2000), 7.

2 C. S. Lewis, *Letters to Malcolm: Chiefly on Prayer* (London: Geoffrey Bles, 1964), 75.

3 Leighton Ford, *The Attentive Life: Discovering God's Presence in All Things* (Downers Grove: InterVarsity Press, 2014).

4 Kevin Vanhoozer, "In Bright Shadow: C.S. Lewis on the Imagination for Theology and Discipleship", *Desiring God*, 28 Sept 2013. https://www.desiringgod.org/messages/in-bright-shadow-c-s-lewis-on-the-imagination-for-theology-and-discipleship, (accessed December 8, 2016).

5 Paula Gooder, *Everyday God: The Spirit of the Ordinary* (Norwich: Canterbury Press, 2012), 134.

6 Ken Gire, *The Reflective Life: Becoming More Spiritually Sensitive to the Everyday Moments of Life* (Eastbourne: Kingsway, 1999), 11.

7 Ruth Hayley Barton, *Strengthening the Soul of Your Leadership: Seeking God in the Crucible of Ministry* (Downers Grove: InterVarsity Press, 2008), 62 and 64.

8 Barbara Brown Taylor, *An Altar in the World: A Geography of Faith* (Norwich: Canterbury Press, 2009), 24.

9 J. Sidlow Baxter, *Explore the Book: Volume 3* (Grand Rapids: Zondervan, 1962), 261.

10 Elizabeth Barrett Browning, "From 'Aurora Leigh'", *Oxford Book of English Mystical Verse*, ed. D. H. S. Nicholson and A. H. E. Lee (Oxford: Oxford University Press, 1917).

11 John R. W. Stott, *God's New Society: The Message of Ephesians* (Downers Grove: InterVarsity Press, 1980), 54.

12 Matthew Henry, *Commentary on the Whole Bible* (London: Marshall, Morgan & Scott, 1961), 284.

13 "The Servant Songs", first identified by German Lutheran scholar Bernhard Duhm, are usually identified as Isaiah 42:1–9, 49:1–6, 50:4–9 and 52:13–53:12.

14 Richard Peace, *Noticing God* (Downers Grove: InterVarsity Press, 2012), 19.

15   Adapted from Elizabeth Ruth Obbard's, *Life in God's NOW: The Sacrament of the Present Moment* (New York City: New City Press, 2012).

16   Ruth Hayley Barton, "Part 1: The Road Between the Now and the Not-Yet", adapted from *Life Together in Christ* (Downers Grove: InterVarsity Press, 2014), *Transforming Center*, 4 April 2015. https://transforming-center.org/2015/04/road-together/, (accessed September, 2017).

17   Jon Bloom, "Cleopas: The Eyes that Are Most Important to Jesus", Desiring God, 1 May 2010, https://www.desiringgod.org/articles/cleopas-the-eyes-that-are-most-important-to-jesus, (accessed September, 2017).

18   Tom Rath, "Vital Friends: The People You Can't Afford to Live Without" (Washington: Gallup Press, 2006), 15, as quoted in Tan Soo-Inn, *Friends in a Broken World* (Singapore: Graceworks, 2008), 9.

19   Aelred of Rievaulx, *Spiritual Friendship* (Collegeville: Cistercian Publications, 2010), 55.

20   Keith R. Anderson, *Reading Your Life's Story: An Invitation to Spiritual Mentoring* (Downers Grove: InterVarsity Press, 2016), 12.

21   Eugene Peterson, *Eat This Book: A Conversation in the Art of Spiritual Reading* (London, Hodder & Stoughton, 2006), 18.

22   Richard Foster, *Life with God: Reading the Bible for Spiritual Transformation* (London, Hodder & Stoughton, 2008), vii.

23   Mary A. Lathbury and Alexander Groves, *Break Thou the Bread of Life* (Psalter Hymnal, 1987).

24   Tish Harrison Warren, *Liturgy of the Ordinary: Sacred Practices in Everyday Life* (Downers Grove: InterVarsity Press, 2016), 71.

25   Brother Lawrence, *The Practice of the Presence of God* (Mineola: Dover Publications, 2005), Kindle.

26   Ibid., Kindle.

❧ Bibliography

Barbara Brown Taylor, *An Altar in the World: A Geography of Faith*, Norwich: Canterbury Press, 2009.

Ben Campbell Johnson, *Living before God: Deepening Our Sense of Divine Presence*, Grand Rapids: Eerdmans, 2000.

David Benner, *Presence and Encounter: The Sacramental Possibilities of Everyday Life*, Ada: Brazos Press, 2014.

Elizabeth Ruth Obbard, *Life in God's NOW: The Sacrament of the Present Moment*, New York City: New City Press, 2012.

Ken Gire, *The Reflective Life: Becoming More Spiritually Sensitive to the Everyday Moments of Life*, Eastbourne: Kingsway, 1998.

Leighton Ford, *The Attentive Life: Discovering God's Presence in All Things*, Downers Grove: InterVarsity Press, 2008.

Paula Gooder, *Everyday God: The Spirit of the Ordinary*, Norwich: Canterbury Press, 2012.

Richard Peace, *Noticing God*, Downers Grove: InterVarsity Press, 2012.

Timothy Jones, *Awake my Soul: Practical Spirituality for Busy People*, New York City: Doubleday, 1999.

Tish Harrison Warren, *Liturgy of the Ordinary: Sacred Practices in Everyday Life*, Downers Grove: InterVarsity Press, 2016.

Charis Training

Charis Training (www.charistraining.co.uk) reflects the teaching ministry of Tony Horsfall. Founded in 2002. Tony is married to Evelyn, and they have two grown-up children. They live in Cudworth, near the town of Barnsley in Yorkshire, England.

It is the aim of Charis Training to enable individuals (and especially those in full-time Christian ministry) to experience the wonderful grace of God in a personal way, and as a result begin to enjoy the kind of intimacy with God that is promised to us in the Bible, and which leads to a fruitful and effective life.

You can contact Tony at *tonyhorsfall@uwclub.net*, or via Facebook and Skype.

GRACEWORKS

Graceworks is a publishing and training consultancy based in Singapore, dedicated to promoting spiritual friendship in church and society, and seeing lives transformed through books that present truth for life.

Our publications can be found on our online store, *www.graceworks.com.sg*. Paperbacks are also available on Bookdepository and Amazon and eBooks on Kindle, iBooks and Kobo.

You can contact us at *enquiries@graceworks.com.sg,* or follow us on Facebook (@GraceworksSG) and Instagram (gracew

Lightning Source UK Ltd.
Milton Keynes UK
UKHW010635190821
389117UK00002B/429